995

SALVATION
AND
LIBERATION

Leonardo and Clodovis Boff

SALVATION
AND
LIBERATION

Translated from the Portuguese
by Robert R. Barr

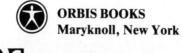
ORBIS BOOKS
Maryknoll, New York

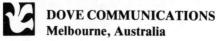
DOVE COMMUNICATIONS
Melbourne, Australia

Third Printing, June 1988

The Catholic Foreign Mission Society of America (Maryknoll) recruits and trains people for overseas missionary service. Through Orbis Books Maryknoll aims to foster the international dialogue that is essential to mission. The books published, however, reflect the opinions of their authors and are not meant to represent the official position of the society.

Originally published as *Da libertação: O sentido teológico das libertações sócio-historicas*, copyright © 1979 Editora Vozes Ltda., Rua Frei Luís, 100, 25.600 Petrópolis, RJ, Brazil

English translation copyright © 1984 Orbis Books, Maryknoll, NY 10545
Published in the United States of America by Orbis Books, Maryknoll, NY 10545
All rights reserved
Manufactured in the United States of America

Manuscript Editor: William E. Jerman

Library of Congress Cataloging in Publication Data
Boff, Leonardo.
  Salvation and liberation.

  Translation of: Da libertação.
  Includes bibliographical references.
  1. Liberation theology. I. Boff, Clodovis.
II. Title.
BT83.57.B613   1984   261.8'098   84-7220
ISBN 0-88344-451-8 (pbk.)

Published in Australia in 1984 by Dove Communications, Box 316 Blackburn, Victoria 3130

Dove ISBN 0-85924-325-7

For
Gustavo Gutiérrez
amicus in veritate
et ex corde
fellow pilgrim

Contents

1

LEONARDO BOFF

Salvation in Liberation: The Theological Meaning of Socio-historical Liberation

The Fundamentals of Liberation Theology

There is a heated discussion in progress on the subject of the theology of liberation. Whenever mental heat is generated and confusion arises, it becomes imperative to return to the simple terms of the original question. What is actually at issue? What is the question underlying liberation theology?

Theological reflection is the result of an effort to understand the root problem. If we fail to grasp the root problem, we shall scarcely understand the theology of liberation springing from it. Hence the importance of being clear about the absolute fundamentals of Latin American reality and Latin American theological reflection upon it, in order to be able to engage in a dialogue on liberation theology.

The Spirituality of the Poor

At the roots of the theology of liberation we find a spirituality, a mysticism: the encounter of the poor with the Lord. Today the poor are a whole class of marginalized and exploited persons in our society, marked as that society is by an exclusive partnership with a dependent capitalism. A theology—any theology—not based on a spiritual experience is mere panting—religious breathlessness. Liberation theology takes its point of departure in the reality of misery described by the bishops at the Puebla meeting of the Latin American Episcopal Council (CELAM):

> [It is] the most devastating and humiliating kind of scourge. And this situation finds expression in such things as a high rate of infant mortality, lack of adequate housing, health problems, starvation wages, unemployment and underemployment, malnutrition, job uncertainty, compulsory mass migrations, etc. [Puebla 29].[1]

Anyone not perceiving this scandalous reality will fail to understand the discourse of the theology of liberation.

This root experience can be developed on two levels: the sensible (how it looks to our eyes at first glance), or the analytical (how it looks in its structural mechanisms exposed to view by scientific analysis). These two ways of "reworking" one and the same experience yield two different types of theology of liberation, with two different "efficacies": the one "sacramental"—because it works with the "signs" by which poverty is manifested—and the other socio-analytical—because it works with the structures underlying these "signs."

"Sacramental" Articulation of Liberation Theology

Perception of Misery (Feeling).   The misery of reality shows us two faces: that of the anguish caused by "hunger, chronic diseases, illiteracy, impoverishment, injustice" (Puebla

26/127), and that of the hopes for liberation, participation, and communion (Puebla 24/127). We realize that we are confronted with a deep division between rich and poor, one all the more painful for us when we know that both profess the same Christian faith.

Ethico-Religious Indignation at Misery (Protest). The first reaction of Christian faith in the face of this reality is protest. This cannot be! This is not pleasing to God! The Puebla Final Document says:

> Viewing it in the light of faith, we see the growing gap between rich and poor as a scandal and a contradiction to Christian existence. The luxury of a few becomes an insult to the wretched poverty of the vast masses. This is contrary to the plan of the Creator and to the honor that is due him [Puebla 28/128].

Solidarity in Praxis: Help (Action). The perception of misery, and protest against that misery, move the Christian conscience to act. The church has always had concern for the poor of our continent. Today this concern has assumed the form of a collective conscience, as the continuation of a like situation grows more and more intolerable.

But the strategy whereby the church comes to the aid of the poor has undergone a change. In times gone by, the church was bound to the dominant classes, and it was through their mediation that the church reached out to the poor, to whom the dominant classes were giving "assistance." The presence of the church was "assistentialistic," paternalistic. The church came to the aid of the poor, it is true, but made no use of the resources of the poor in instituting a process of change. Now the church goes directly to the poor, joining them in their struggles, and forming basic communities where faith is vibrant and alive in its social and liberating dimension. Accordingly, the presence of the church in society is no longer effectuated merely by religious practice in the strict sense (in devotional or liturgical practice). It has become a matter of joining to religious practices ethical and social ones as well, practices concerned with the promotion and advancement of "the whole human being and all human beings."

These practices are demanded by the Christian faith itself. After all, that faith becomes *genuine* faith, faith that saves, only when it is (as philosophers say) "informed" by love, only when love becomes "of the very essence" of that faith. But love is praxis, not theory. Faith without the practice of love is empty faith, not the faith that leads to the kingdom of God.

Socio-Analytical Articulation of Liberation Theology

On this level of development we meet with a need for a critical knowledge of the mechanisms that produce misery. Misery is not innocent. It does not come out of nowhere. The Puebla bishops' observation is on the mark:

> Analyzing this situation more deeply, we discover that this poverty is not a passing phase. Instead it is the product of economic, social, and political situations and structures, though there are also other causes for the state of misery. In many instances this state of poverty within our countries finds its origin and support in mechanisms which, because they are impregnated with materialism rather than any authentic humanism, create a situation on the international level where the rich get richer at the expense of the poor, who get ever poorer [Puebla 30/128].

The principal interest of liberation theology is to generate activity on the part of the church that will aid the poor *efficaciously.* Everything must converge toward practice (love). The real question is: What praxis will *actually,* and not just seemingly, be of help? Good will is not enough here. Lucidity is needed. You can jump into the river to save your drowning friend, and this shows your good will. In fact, it shows your love. But if you have never learned to swim, you do not save your friend. On the contrary, the two of you die together. Love you certainly had. But it was not a very intelligent love, and it was totally inefficacious, ineffective.

How can we bestow efficacity on Christian love? The key is to know reality better—to understand better the mechanisms that produce poverty, and the avenues that can lead its victims away from it. And here we speak of the "three mediations" of liberation theology. A "mediation," here, is a *means* with which this theology is endowed for bringing to realization what it proposes to itself as an end. The theology of liberation is possessed of three mediations: the socio-analytical, the hermeneutic, and that of pastoral practice.

We work with instruments calculated to improve our perception of "contradictory reality," so as to overcome the ingenuousness, the empiricism, and the moralism that prevent us from acquiring a critical knowledge of this reality: this is the *socio-analytical mediation.*

Next, we have to go deeper than just our ethical-Christian indignation in the face of socio-political contradictions. Prophetic cries, necessary though they may be (for it is they that unleash action), fail to modify reality, nor are they any guarantee of the correct interpretation of reality in the light of faith. Interpretation is the task of the *hermeneutic mediation.*

Finally, we have to search out the viable, sensible avenues down which the liberation of the poor can travel, within the framework of religious, political, military, ideological, and economic forces, and so on, that exist within society. And this is the *mediation of pastoral practice.*

As can be seen, the theology of liberation is genuine theology only when it takes basic experience—in its various stages, as we have considered above—and reworks it on a more critical and careful level. Let us examine each of these basic mediations.

Socio-Analytical Mediation: Seeing. Reality has to be grasped critically if one hopes to be able to affect it more efficaciously in the name of our faith. We can point to three levels of awareness of reality, with three corresponding forms of action upon this reality.

Empiricism moves from (1) the facts to (2) a naive awareness to (3) assistentialism. I am struck by the degrees of poverty among our population. I draw up a list of the clamoring facts and am scandalized. And there I stick. I fail to go beyond the factual dimension. I fail to go to the deeper causes, which are generally invisible.

This attitude, which is sometimes a noble one and always full of good will, we call empiricism. A person has a naive awareness of the facts, a naive conscience, and his or her activity, normally, will be assistentialistic. He or she attends to the facts as they present themselves. All good will aside, one must ask oneself whether this is the best manner of coming to know a situation and aiding those in need. Certainly it is not, as we see from the limited scope of the resulting action. It supplies you with a pond, but does not teach you to fish.

Functionalism proceeds from (1) socio-economic circumstances to (2) a critical consciousness to (3) reformism. This analytical posture not only sees the facts; it sees how they are interrelated, how they form a "conjuncture." Society is like a body, in which many functions are being performed, and these functions must work together in an organic way, creating social harmony. When there is dysfunction, as is the case with too great a gulf between rich and poor, reforms must be implemented, so that the less developed, the "underdeveloped," part of the body, will develop, thus reestablishing social equilibrium.

With functionalism, awareness of reality is a critical awareness. Account is taken of the interrelationship of everything in society with everything else. The function of the state is to administer the common welfare, the function of the church is to pray, that of the worker is to work, that of the business person is to see to profits, that of the teacher is to teach, and so forth. If everything functions well, problems do not arise.

The ideal of functionalism is admirable. Yet the real question is left out of account: Why, in the form of society in which we live, do the poor grow ever poorer and the rich ever richer, in spite of the considerable industrial progress we see all around us? Devel-

opment is development for whom? And by whom is it effectuated? And with what means is it constructed? A more critical
analysis will be able to demonstrate that development in capitalist
molds is effectuated at the cost of the people, and generally
against the people. Progress benefits only some strata of the population, marginalizing broader sectors.

Functionalism, with its developmentalism and progressivism,
does not succeed in making society function with humanly admis-
sible and bearable relationships in terms of justice and participation. The social tax of inequality levied by modern progress is
immense, and is paid by the common masses. The questions we
have raised above are not adequately answered by functionalism.
They call for another approach.

There was a time when the great majority of the pastoral ministers in the church were to be found within this analytical camp.
Enthusiastically they summoned the people to progress, and faith
bolstered the will to development. But in the measure that these
pastoral ministers identified with the people, and entered into the
lifestyle of the people, they came to grasp that progress was being
made at the cost of the people, and that it marginalized the people
more and more. The social system was found to be vitiated as a
system, and not merely in its "conjunctures." It was not just ill, it
was terminally ill.

Dialectical structuralism moves from (1) structure to (2) a radical critical awareness to (3) liberation. This analytical posture is
not content with examining conjunctures. It goes into a deeper
analysis and uncovers the global structure of the system. It examines how this system organizes our society in capitalistic
molds. In the words of *Populorum Progressio*:

> [It is] a system . . . which considers profit as the key motive
> for economic progress, competition as the supreme law of
> economics, and private ownership of the means of produc-
> tion as an absolute right that has no limits and carries
> no corresponding social obligation [*Populorum Progressio,*
> no. 26].[2]

Obviously, faced with new historical conjunctures, capitalism has modified its game-rules. But never its game—never its system. The principal contradiction of this "woeful system" (*Populorum Progressio,* no. 26 ³) lies in the fact that all, by their labor, contribute to the production of goods, but only certain ones—those who hold capital—acquire ownership of these goods, to the exclusion of the others.

We call this analysis "structuralist" because it rests on a consideration of the structure underlying both conjunctures and concrete facts. The latter are adequately understood only when we grasp the capitalistic structure of our society. We call it "dialectical" structuralism because of the difficult and conflictive interaction prevailing between those who hold capital and the rest of society, which constitutes the labor force. An analysis of the interplay of these forces gives the investigator to understand the makeup, evolution, and perpetuation of the type of society that is ours.

The consciousness, the awareness, that grasps these links, these articulations, is called "radical criticism." It is called "radical," not in the buzzword sense of being polarized on the "left," but because it goes to the "roots" (Latin, *radices*) of the question. The therapy prescribed by this radical criticism, or radical critique, is not the reform of the system. This would be applying a palliative to the ulcer without getting down to the source of the illness. Radical criticism calls for a new form of organization for the whole of society, an organization on other bases—no longer from a point of departure of the capital held in the hands of a few, but an organization of society based on everyone's labor, with everyone sharing, in the means and the goods of production as well as in the means of power. And this is called liberation.

The theology of liberation starts with this type of reading of social reality—a radical criticism, a dialectical structuralism. This is the analysis that reveals to the investigator the *ongoing* mechanisms of poverty and marginalization.

Hermeneutic Mediation: Judging. Hermeneutics is the science and technique of interpretation by means of which we are enabled to understand the original meaning of any writings (or realities) no longer *immediately* comprehensible to men and women of today. For example, hermeneutics interprets the Christian scriptures and the more important documents preserved in tradition. Between us and the Bible, more than two thousand years intervene. Mentalities have changed, and words have acquired new meanings. How can we comprehend the word of God, which is meant to be the light to guide all our actions, if this word is incarnate in a lost mentality and a lost language? Evidently, we must build a bridge. That is, we must interpret. Hence we speak of a hermeneutic mediation.

By means of the hermeneutic mediation we develop the theological criteria with which we intend to read a text—in this case, the socio-analytical "text" of reality. Only thus is social reality, with its contradictions, "appropriated" by theology, and a page is turned in the history of religion. What is God trying to tell us in these social problems, now adequately grasped by scientific reason? This is the challenge. Reason is not enough here. Enter . . . faith.

By faith, scripture, and tradition (the teaching of the church, the *sensus fidelium,* the teaching of the theologians, and so on), we verify the presence or absence of God in reality. We identify a response to God's salvific design or its rejection. Where social analysis says "structural poverty," faith will say "structural sin." Where analysis says "private accumulation of wealth," faith will say "sin of selfishness."

In sum: the task of theology with respect to social reality is discharged on three levels. The *first level* is that of the evaluation of a situation in terms of salvation history. In the light of categories of faith such as kingdom of God, salvation, perdition, grace, sin, justice, injustice, charity, and so on, this or that society is found to be orientated toward God's design, or not so orientated. This is the prophetic moment of theology.

The *second level* is that of a reading, in terms of a liberating critique or criticism, of our faith-tradition itself. Does a given interpretation of kingdom, grace, church, sin, and human activ-

ity finish by involuntarily abetting or legitimating exactly what
they are intended to overcome—so deep a cleft between rich and
poor? We know that the faith and the church have been utilized
by the powerful. Further, there is a "bilingualism" to be avoided.
That is, one must not construct a theological discourse that
manages to run parallel to the socio-analytic discourse without
ever touching it. Each must proceed in conjunction with the
other, so that a theology is developed that succeeds, that is efficacious, in interpreting—in the light of the word of God and
tradition—social reality, especially the social reality of the poor.

The *third level* is a theological reading of the whole of human
activity, that of Christians as well as that of non-Christians. In
other words, theology must not be restricted to an analysis of the
liberating praxis of Christians. It knows that God is rejected or
asserted whenever and wherever justice is denied or maintained, a
communion of brothers and sisters is realized or not, and the like.
Hence it pertains to theology to speak out on any and every practice or form of social intercourse.

The Christian faith develops its picture of the human being and
of society from the future, from the ultimate destiny of history.
The Christian conception is not totally exhaustible in political
practice. Neither can it be reduced to a particular form of society.
But Christian faith helps the Christian make an option, among
the de facto concretions of history, for this or that particular analysis of reality. For example, Christian faith helps a person choose
a particular instrument of social analysis as being the better way
to unmask the mechanisms that are the vehicles of injustice and
violence, especially against the poor.

Again, faith helps the Christian endorse and support those historical movements that have a greater affinity with the ideals of
the gospel. Today, for example, we perceive that the Christian
ideal is closer to socialism than to capitalism. It is not a matter of
creating a Christian socialism. It is a matter of being able to say
that the socialist system, when actually carried out in reality, enables Christians better to live the humanitarian and divine ideals
of their faith. These ideals *can* also be realized in the capitalist

system, as we see from centuries of Christianity lived by a capitalist society. But the capitalist system is attended by many contradictions that could be overcome in another system—which for its part will present other contradictions, but lesser ones.

Mediation of Pastoral Practice: Acting. In the third mediation we address the translation into concrete action of what has previously been seen and assessed, or judged. How should we go about this? We must situate ourselves on a different level from that of social analysis or theology—the procedures of the first two mediations. We have, then, an epistemological rupture to undertake, for action has laws different from those of analysis and reflection.

First, we must take account of the total play of social forces—economic, political, ideological, repressive—in order not to fall victim to a naive voluntarism. As a general rule, we do not do what we wish to; we do what objective conditions of reality permit us to do. This is where pastoral prudence enters the scene. It is not a matter of yielding to intimidation, but of exercising wisdom with respect to what is feasible and viable.

Next, it is important to identify, in the complex of economic, political, and symbolical reality, the specific initiative of the church. That is, it is important to identify how the church, from a point of departure in its identity as seen in the light of faith, can perform liberating activity. As the institutionalized community of faith, the church occupies a position within the symbolical instance, a position on the level of sign. In the social totality, it does not play a determining role, but it does play a very important one—especially in the Latin American context, where it carries considerable historical and social weight.

It is in its symbolical capacity, then, that the church has the duty to act as agent of liberation. It must attempt to articulate its word, its catechesis, its liturgy, its community action, and its interventions with established authority, in the direction of liberation. The faith possesses an unequaled dimension for liberation, and this dimension has constant need of being recovered and kept alive.

Further, the church will have to join and interact with other social forces that are also in quest of qualitative change. Only thus will the efficacy desired by the church be attained with reasonable ease. It is not only the church that seeks liberation—although it is the church that must ever maintain the totalizing perspective of integral liberation (that of the kingdom of God), unlike other groups, which are restricted in their aim and rationale to socio-historical liberation.

Finally, Christians, and Christian organizations, where such exist or are to exist, can and should, without involving ecclesiastical authority on the official level, seek out a complexus of activity that is not limited merely to the area of the symbolic. They may and must, in the name of their Christian faith and conscience, act on the directly political and infrastructural level. It is on this level that we can visualize a relative autonomy for basic Christian communities. By reason of their nature as basic, they are more directly concerned with problems of liberation, so that for them the concrete opposition faced by liberation efforts becomes more urgent, and its resolution better defined.

The strategic definition of liberation must always remain clear, even when, by dint of historical conjunctures, we are obliged to settle for merely reformist measures. Liberation, by definition, involves a qualitatively new society. Reformist measures are only tactical steps, not strategic goals. These measures, these steps, must point to, and serve, liberation. Liberation is never merely a matter of intention, aspiration. It is the fruit of a process, in which all must participate; it is not the result of a single stroke of the will.

Liberation as Messianic Task

The theology of liberation has been built fundamentally on the basis of these three mediations.[4] Each mediation has its problems. But all constitute moments in a single dialectical movement, which is faith in search of efficacy and lucidity, in solidarity with the oppressed. If we violate this unity, we fall victim either to sociologism and politicization, or to theologism, or even to pastoral pragmatism.

The critical point seems to me to reside mostly in the first moment, that of the socio-analytical interpretation of historico-social reality, and less in the second and third (theology and pastoral action). Not all of us are possessed of the same level of awareness of the conflicts in socio-political reality. Hence our analyses diverge, so that we then make different theological readings, and finally adopt different types of action. Tensions within the church are not typically the outgrowth of problems of faith. Much more often they are generated by problems connected with different stances taken up vis-à-vis social reality.

Finally, liberation theology seeks to articulate a reading of reality from the perspective of the poor, in the concern for their liberation. Motivated by this basic stance, this theology then utilizes the human and social sciences, projects theological mediations, and calls for pastoral activities calculated to foster the progress of the oppressed, aiding them on their journey.

For the faith and its tradition, the mission of delivering the victims of injustice and marginalization is ascribed to the Messiah. The messianic community is joined to this task in its capacity as sign and instrument of integral liberation. Through the theology of liberation, that community seeks to make adequate critical response to the basic question exercising our Christian and Latin American conscience: How can we be Christians in a world of misery? We can be Christians, authentic Christians, only by living our faith in a liberating way.

2

LEONARDO BOFF

Integral Liberation and Partial Liberations

With its consecration of the liberation thematic in its Final Document, Puebla erected an unshakable framework for theology and the church in Latin America. The task of theology is now to endow a liberating practice and a liberating reflection with mutual cohesiveness. In the following pages, then, I shall attempt to resituate, in the light of Puebla, the problematic arising from the theological meaning of socio-historical liberations.

Atmosphere of Liberation

The liberation theme made its appearance in Latin America, especially in Brazil, in the early 1960s, in the context of an analysis of the phenomenon of underdevelopment.

Two interpretations of underdevelopment had been thrust aside, judged as inadequate or erroneous: underdevelopment as technological lag (in "developing" countries), and underdevelopment as the result of the (unequal) interdependence of parts in a single system (a system of developed and underdeveloped countries). The outcome was a more adequate interpretation, one that understood underdevelopment as the other face of development—as a system of dependency on hegemonic centers. Underdevelopment was now seen not merely as a matter of "develop*ing* countries," nor even as a matter of a system of "developed *and* underdeveloped countries." Underdevelopment had come to be seen as a matter of *countries maintained in a state of underdevelopment.*

The most enlightening categories of this correlation of opposition were those of dependency versus liberation. Each of these categories implied an analysis and at the same time a denunciation. Dependency denotes a system of oppression calling for ethical indignation. Liberation means action delivering a captive to liberty and calling for a humanistic commitment.

Reflection on Liberating Practices

This new interpretation was not content to stay on the level of theoretical discussion. It began to penetrate praxis. It began to "inform" practices already underway, with an eye to a process of liberation—from a point of departure in the poor especially, with their values, and their revolutionary potential.[5] The agent of social transformation should be the people itself, in conjunction with strata organically associated with the people, and not the dominant elite. The *Movimento de Educação de Base* ["movement for basic education"], *Ação Popular* ["popular action"], and Paulo Freire's educational method as a praxis of freedom and a pedagogy of the oppressed would be examples. In a word, the people should be involved with movements constituting a "libertarian atmosphere." [6]

In these same movements linked with liberation there were a goodly number of Christians and pastoral ministers, especially in *Ação Operária Católica* ["Catholic worker action"], *Juventude Universitária Católica* ["Catholic university youth"], and *Juven-*

tude Estudantil Católica ["Catholic student youth"]. Theological reflection was pursued in those circles apropos of the new problematic of dependency and liberation. Account was taken of the inadequacy of the theology of development and of the limitations of a theology of revolution. New vistas opened with the advent of a theology of liberation.

Those Christians and pastoral ministers were involved in liberating practices, with a view to creating the conditions for the rupture that had to take place in society. Their theological reflection was not being done primarily to justify those practices, any more than it was done in order to be able to deduce the authenticity of particular libertarian commitments and involvement. They were doing their theology based on practices that were being experienced and lived jointly with other persons who were not necessarily Christians. Their commitment to the poor, made for political motives, elucidated by an analysis of the process of underdevelopment, now had some questions to ask the Christian faith.

Christians began to wonder: What is the function of our Christian faith within our politico-ideological option? Does it function as a brake, a restraint? Or is it a spur? Or, finally, is Christian faith neutral with respect to the struggle for liberation? It is easy to see that these concrete practices opened a new eye to the content of the faith and the scriptures, and this eye was gazing most intently.

A great number of Christians were rediscovering the libertarian dimensions of their faith. Some points were emerging as particularly revealing. There was the matter of the poor in Matthew 25:35-46, the parable of the last judgment. There was the theme of exodus and deliverance, exodus and liberation. There was the conception of faith as salvific only if it passes by way of the praxis of love—Matthew 7:21-23 ("Many will plead with me, 'Lord, Lord' . . ."). There was Jesus' option for the abandoned and marginalized of his time, and the conflictive character of his life and death as a consequence of a liberation praxis. There was the message of the kingdom as already beginning to be realized here in history, and the unity of history seen in the light of salvation or perdition, oppression or liberation—the attainment of one's ultimate end in God or its absolute frustration, and the dependence of all this on one's manner of life here on earth. And there was many another appropriate biblical subject for theological reflection.[7]

Faith emerged not as a brake, but indeed a spur, a moving force. This was the context, in the mid-1960s, of the first deeper reflections of what would later be called the theology of liberation. Inasmuch as the problems were mainly economic, political, and educational, what Christians tried to see was the theological relevance of their commitment in the area of economic, political, and educational liberation. Does economic and political liberation not have a theological dimension? If it does, then a commitment on the part of Christians to economics and politics involves a commitment to God, to the kingdom, to salvation.

It is important to keep this perspective in view: the struggle for economic, political, and educational liberation goes beyond the scope of these areas. They have a theological dimension. Besides concretizing sociological liberation as such, they concretize the liberation given by God. In other words, in these realities, considered to be secular, there is a real, but hidden, theological element. Only faith enables one to see this element present within the economic, the political, and the educational. It is the task of Christian reflection to unveil and extract this hidden theological element, to bring it to the light of day in reflection, in liturgical celebration, in an expression of prayer.

On this level, integral liberation was not yet the subject of discourse. Liberation from sin, from deviant interior attitudes, and the like, was simply presupposed as already belonging to the solid, sure treasury of Christian faith. It was not discussed. But silence was not denial. What was already known and received was not discussed. What was discussed was this new vision: God's liberation is present within the historical liberation of human beings.

What enabled Christians to discern the concealed theological component of these manifestly secular realities?[8] The contributions of the theology of the thirty years before Vatican II, which were adopted by Vatican II, played a large role: the view of salvation history as a single plan on the part of God. God's self-donation is offered to human beings in their history, wherever there may be human beings. No man or woman can escape the word of God. All persons hear that word at all times, and their every action expresses acceptance or rejection of God and God's grace. Hence all dimensions of history—the economic, the political, and so on—are surely also elements in God's design. In them, human beings answer yes or no to God, in the measure that they are willing to be the vehicles of justice, of a community of sisters and brothers, and of benevolent mutual encounters—or in the measure that they are the instruments of domination, of breach, and of structural injustice.

Accordingly, a more explicitly biblical outlook with respect to God's plan, expressed in the category of salvation (or perdition) history, was now joined to a theological anthropology that saw the human being as a historical being permanently open to the Transcendent, and giving, from within his or her concrete life situation, an answer to God: yes or no. This helped persons to perceive God and God's grace beyond the limits of the language that speaks of them overtly.

A deeper understanding of eschatology led to a better understanding of salvation and of the process of its concretization in history. Salvation defines the terminal situation of the human being in God. It was secured once and for all by the redemptive act of Jesus Christ. But salvation is not actualized only in the last moment of one's life, or only in eternity. It is anticipated. The human being must enter upon a whole salvation process, a process that begins here on earth and ends in eternity.

This process, which gradually actualizes salvation within the limits of history, especially within the space of the church, can be understood as a process of liberation *from* situations that contradict God's salvific design, *for* situations that gradually conform to that design. Historical liberations are thus anticipations and concretizations, ever limited, but real, of the salvation that will be full and complete only in eternity.

This vision has permitted a theological reading of human efforts in the molding of more just and more humane situations. In proportion as economic and social structures foster a greater participation by all in the economy and in society and create a greater symmetry among groups of persons, in that same proportion they signify, to the eyes of faith, the presence of grace and the realization, in seed, of the kingdom of God. When, on the contrary, they generate exploitation and impoverishment, they reveal the presence of sin and the antikingdom.

I do not intend to linger on this point. I wish only to emphasize the principal theological points of reference that enable us to see God and God's kingdom where otherwise they would remain anonymous—within economic and political processes.

Global Discourse on Liberation

From a point of departure in this "regional" theology—this theology circumscribed by the limits of the economic and political "regions" (in other words, by concrete history)—we eventually witnessed a theological soaring to higher plateaus, accompanied by the danger of losing the density and concreteness of discourse upon socio-political processes. This was the discourse on integral liberation: liberation from all servitudes, liberation from sin. As early as the 1966 CELAM meeting in Mar del Plata, Argentina, Dom Hélder Câmara could say:

> The goal to be attained is that of being a free and conscientious being, in a progressive liberation from a thousand servitudes, in order that our basic freedom may grow: in order that we may be free to the point of being able to deliver ourselves from ourselves and be able to give ourselves to others.[9]

This is a statement of the global discourse on liberation. And it is valid, beyond any shadow of a doubt. But faith and tradition had always known and proclaimed it. The theological discourse on economics, politics, and education was what was new.

The CELAM conference held in Medellín in 1968 took up the thematic of liberation and made it one of its key topics. Predominant was the perspective of integral liberation, which included political liberation, but the accent fell on liberation from sin and the consequences of sin: "the liberation of the entire human being and of all human beings." What was new in the Medellín perspective was subsumed in a perspective that was, in itself, traditional. At all events, Medellín had the merit of consecrating, on the official church level, the discourse on liberation, and of thus lending the support of its authority to the liberating practices already undertaken by Christians who were socially involved.

After Medellín, the liberation discourse multiplied prolifically, with a most exuberant literary output. There was an amazing variety of approaches. We heard the liberation discourse on every wavelength—and thereby, of course, the real need of the moment was slighted: reflection on the relationship between salvation in Jesus Christ and the processes of historical liberation. What theological relevance was embodied in the liberation process currently underway under the auspices of groups committed to change in society, especially in the popular sectors?

There is, then, a liberation process. There are many persons involved, of various ideological hues, including many Christians. And so the question is asked: How is this process related to the salvation offered by Jesus Christ? Is there a difference between them? What is the difference? Or are they the same thing? Or have they simply no connection with each other at all? Is there an articulation, a set of connections, between them? What is the nature of this articulation? These were the theological questions that emerged in theological reflection during the period between Medellín and Puebla—questions that are still being asked today.

Medellín undertook no reflection on these questions. The relationship between liberation and salvation was still conceived along the lines of *Gaudium et Spes* (especially paragraph 39), where the emphasis is more on their unity than on their distinction:[10]

> As all liberation is already an anticipation of full redemption in Christ, the church in Latin America feels a particular solidarity with any educational effort tending to the liberation of our peoples [Medellín, Education, 9].

It was in the context of this problematic that Paul VI published *Evangelii Nuntiandi,* in 1975. The very first section is devoted to the question of the interrelationship of liberation and evangelization. The pope's central concern is to express this interrelationship without separating the two terms, but also without identifying them. Then, after referring to the abundant evidence as to the misery of millions of human beings, the pope proclaims his basic thesis:

> The church . . . has the duty to proclaim the liberation of millions of human beings, many of whom are her own children. . . . This is not foreign to evangelization [*Evangelii Nuntiandi,* no. 30].[11]

If it is not foreign to evangelization, how is it related to it?

First the pope condemns two reductionisms—on the political side and on the religious side. On the political side: the church is not willing "to reduce her mission to the dimensions of a simply temporal project" (no. 32). On the religious side: "the church is certainly not willing to restrict her mission only to the religious field and dissociate herself from man's temporal problems" (no. 34). As we see, the problem consists in the interrelationship of the political with the religious:

> The church links human liberation and salvation in Jesus Christ, but she never identifies them, because she knows through revelation, historical experience, and the reflection

of faith that not every notion of liberation is necessarily consistent and compatible with an evangelical vision of man, of things and of events [no. 35].

What are the ties providing the possibility of a relationship? The text of the apostolic exhortation itself identifies three:

[There are] links of an *anthropological* order, because the [person] who is to be evangelized is not an abstract being but is subject to social and economic questions. [There are] links in the *theological* order, since one cannot dissociate the plan of creation from the plan of redemption. . . . [There are] links of the eminently evangelical order, which is that of *charity:* how in fact can one proclaim the new commandment without promoting in justice and in peace the true, authentic advancement of man? [no. 31; italics added].

The avenues indicated by the pope are genuinely good ones and can shed light on the complexus of ties, of "links," between Jesus' salvation and the process of liberation, or the "advancement of humankind." But the papal document goes no further into the matter. (This is indeed the task of theology.) However, it sketches the essential frame of reference. Two basic assertions on the part of the pope show the direction in which the interrelationship in question is to be sought:

Salvation is offered to all . . . a transcendent and eschatological salvation, which indeed has its beginning in this life but which is fulfilled in eternity [no. 27].

And again:

The church strives always to insert the Christian struggle for liberation into the universal plan of salvation which she herself proclaims [no. 38; cf. no. 9].

But the actual connection between the two terms of the relationship must be demonstrated, not merely asserted.

In October 1976, the International Theological Commission published the conclusions of its two years of study on the relationship between human advancement and Christian salvation.[12] The problem I have posed was the object of special attention. However, readers will look in vain for a way toward a solution. The material fell far short of the theological level reached by the liberation theologians of Latin America. The discourse is instead full of sidesteps, weaving in and out, vagueness—a discourse more like that of curial ideologues than of serious Catholic theologians involved in doing theology, whose purpose is to generate ideas.

Precisely with reference to the subject in question—the relationship between the liberation process and salvation in Jesus Christ—the authors fail to present any argumentation. They hide behind the authoritative texts of Vatican II, especially *Gaudium et Spes* and *Apostolicam Actuositatem*. They use the argument from authority. This is the easiest and simplest way, of course, but it is also indicative of intellectual sloth. The authors only shuffle terms. Liberation and human advancement should neither be separated nor identified; monism and dualism are equally to be avoided. They shift the problem to others instead of going into it more deeply themselves:

> These problems ought to be subjected to research and new analyses. Beyond a doubt, this constitutes one of the principal tasks of theology today. . . . The definition of this relationship, by its very nature, remains in suspense.[13]

Their document fails to advance the state of the question. On the contrary, it suffers from several basic imprecisions regarding theses of the theology of liberation, as has been pointed out rather sharply by the Spanish theologian José Ignacio González Faus.[14]

The years 1976 to 1979 were turbulent ones for liberation theology in Latin America. In Europe, as interest increased, the first criticisms appeared with regard to various aspects of that theology—its method, its actual or potential utilization of the instrument of Marxist analysis, the linkage between this type of theology and the socialist program. The critics did not always have sufficient information at hand to guarantee the quality of ᵗheir critique. Often they imputed theological error or ambiguity to liberation theology—error and ambiguity that had no connection with it.

In Latin America, meanwhile, this type of theology penetrated deeper and deeper into the grassroots. The General Secretariat of CELAM became the tool of a well-organized campaign against certain liberation theologians. An atmosphere of intrigue and allegation formed, to some extent in all camps. Still, pastoral theology continued to be elaborated. Nearly everything of this description produced in Latin America during those three years falls into the category of theology of liberation. A pastoral practice of liberation knew its first martyrs and confessors—the cruel tribute levied by repression for the commitment of so many pastoral ministers—from lay persons to bishops—to the poor, the evicted, the Amerindians, the exploited.

Variety of Accents, but Only One Liberation Theology

A purely academic and didactic interest will discern various accents within the one, single theology of liberation. I must insist that there is one, and only one, theology of liberation. There is only one point of departure—a reality of social misery—and one goal—the liberation of the oppressed. In a discussion of mediations, accents will vary. It is on this latter level that a variety of tendencies can be discerned—which does not, however, consti· tute alternative liberation theologies.

This observation is important, because, especially in the European discussion, there is much emphasis on an alleged multiplicity of theologies of liberation, in conflict with one another, some in conformity with official standards and others not. Behind such allegations often lurks a mere recourse to ideology, masking the true interests of a theology that refuses to accept being called to account—asked to explain its stance on problems of justice on the international level, or asked to defend its purely academic character, which not infrequently conceals a political naivety and removes from discussion any question as to just what makes theology theology.

What makes theology a Christian theology? Is it only its reference to the "fonts" of the faith—scripture and tradition? Must it not have a conscientious and critical relationship with reality and its conflicts? The statement that a pluralism prevails within the theology of liberation is an easy route to the mechanisms of excuse by which one seeks to exempt oneself from any obligation to answer the questions that this type of theology raises, and thus to write off its validity and legitimacy.

The common point of departure of all the various tendencies within the one theology of liberation is ethical indignation at the misery of social reality, and the demand for a process of liberation that will overcome this contradiction. But there are different ways of developing this basic experience, and this is where a variety of accents can be identified. A brief sketch of the major ones follows.

A *liberation spirituality* is the spiritual moment that gives rise to the theology of liberation. In contact with the poor, who constitute a whole exploited social class, a person experiences a genuine encounter with the Lord and makes a commitment to justice, which is the prime characteristic of the kingdom of God. The themes of poverty, justice, exodus, the following of Christ, the cross as the price of all authentic liberation, resurrection as triumph over injustice, the Easter church, and other themes along these same lines constitute the axes of articulation of a spirituality of liberation. Just as no social revolution lacks its political mystique, so there is no integral religious liberation that is not called forth, animated, and accompanied by a burning mystique of its own—an ardent spirituality.

A *liberative rereading of the scriptures* is another accent. It takes its point of departure in a perception of the real situation of the poor, and, with new eyes, bestowed by this experience, it re-

reads the foundational texts of the faith, the Christian scriptures. Everything there that is relevant for the dimension of liberation is singled out for emphasis and discussion, for reflection and assimilation: the people itself that produced these scriptural texts, as a people oppressed, squeezed, crushed between the great powers of the Middle East and Egypt; the exodus thematic; the exile; messianic liberation; the figure of Jesus of Nazareth as liberator, in a historical and transhistorical time; his message of the kingdom of God as total liberation of human beings and all creation; the cross and resurrection as paschal mystery and paradigm of any process of authentic liberation; the preferential option for the poor on the part of the historical Jesus and the Apostles; conversion as breach with a world sufficient unto itself, and an opening up to the liberating novelty of the kingdom.

From its point of departure in the anguish of the poor of this world, the whole biblical message emerges as a proclamation of liberation. Only from this point of departure among the humiliated and the wronged does the gospel appear as good news. A reading of the scriptures from the viewpoint of the interests of the mighty of this world, or even from that of the interests of those who share in the benefits of civilization, too easily glosses over or "spiritualizes" the vector of liberation that spans the Bible from one end to the other. This rereading from the viewpoint of the poor and the justice due them is very much the practice in the basic Christian communities and constitutes the principal factor in the renewal of biblical studies in Latin America—on a critical level of commitment to the liberating pilgrimage of our churches.

A *rereading of the liberation content in theology* is still another current in Latin American liberation theology. It too begins with a perception of the reality of a people in misery. But instead of undertaking an analysis of the mechanisms of this misery, it immediately engages in a rereading of the content of theology where this content has to do with liberation. All themes in theology have a social and utopian dimension, which, in a socio-political context, must be recovered and placed in the service of the liberation process. Thus one can reread, using liberation as one's hermeneutical key, the mystery of God, of Christ, of the church, of grace and sin, the sacraments, eschatology, anthropology, and mariology. Some significant work has already appeared in Latin America in an attempt to rethink, in systematic fashion, the traditional themes of theology in the interest of the liberation of the oppressed.

Theological reflection on an analysis of reality can incline in various directions. First—and this is the most original and basic current of liberation theology—it can lean toward a critical understanding of the mechanisms that produce oppression. In this instance the prime result will be an *eagerness for liberation.* First, adequate use is made of the instrumentality of the social and human sciences for an analysis of de facto reality. Then, once this has been carried out, the reality thus analyzed is interpreted in the light of faith (using scripture, tradition, the magisterium, and theological reasoning), and God's design, or its absence, is discerned in this reality. Last, from the combination of these two procedures—the scientific analysis and the faith interpretation— paths for pastoral action are derived, with a view to modifying reality in the direction of a greater freedom for the oppressed and the molding of a society that will be more just and thereby more in conformity with the imperatives of the kingdom of God. Here the consuming desire of the people for liberation is taken up in a special way, and the church, in its own way, joins and helps the people in this global process.

But theological reflection on an analysis of reality can also incline toward the perception of *a people's potential for resistance.* The steps are the same as in the preceding approach, but the accent is different. Instead of being on an eagerness for liberation, emphasis is on the people's strength to resist the captivity to which it has been subjected for all these centuries. Here again, there is no question of an alternative theology of liberation: it is merely a matter of recognizing the fact that, despite all oppression, the people still has the strength to resist. It has been able to create what we might call "freedom cells"—for instance in its popular piety, its capacity for celebration, and the like. It has managed to maintain a minimal degree of social cohesion—for example in popular organizations, a certain group effort on farmlands, and so on. And there has never been a time when the people was not in revolt somewhere! Though defeated, it has never dropped the torch of freedom or lost the determination to create a different society.

The people as agent of its own liberation is another theme, reflecting the fact that it is the oppressed themselves who are the proper subject of their own deliverance from oppression. Their popular culture especially, their piety, their organizational forms (such as the basic community), are all factors for conscientization (consciousness-raising) and thrusts for liberation. The theology of liberation engages in a serious study of popular piety in depth. This piety, this religiousness, is not merely a force for resistance; it can also be an important factor for mobilization for social transformation. The intellectual element—the clergy, pastoral ministers—must function in "organic articulation" with these bases. They must allow the people to create new institutional forms of church organization, new religious symbols, and a new incarnation of the gospel in the subordinate classes.

A *popular pedagogy of liberation* makes enormous use of the contributions of the Brazilian educator Paulo Freire, author of *Pedagogy of the Oppressed*.[15] The goal is to enable persons to discover by themselves the paths of their own liberation. This is brought about by helping a people to come to an appreciation of the value of its culture and the power of the poor in history. Here, catechetics and pastoral praxis are especially important vehicles. Without the concrete exercise of praxes of participation, democracy, and liberation, no society of liberated and free persons can arise.

A *rereading of history from the viewpoint of the defeated* constitutes a Latin American project of great earnestness and scope today. What is aimed for is a revision of historical consciousness. Until now, this consciousness has been erected and structured upon the ideology of the dominant classes who have "made it to the top'' and who have done away with memory in the vanquished. That is, the winners have killed memory in the losers, so that now everyone's consciousness of history is that of the victors. A preferential option for the poor enables us to pursue a rereading of history from the standpoint of the Amerindians, slaves, and other marginalized groups.

This approach is uncovering new sources, permitting new interpretations, and unexpectedly coming upon outlooks and viewpoints very different from the major events and phenomena in the history of our Latin American peoples as official interpretation would have it. The purpose of this endeavor is to give our peoples a genuine historical consciousness, without which they will remain rootless and deprived of the support needed to nourish their struggle for liberation. The *Nova História da Igreja na América Latina,* in thirteen volumes, is the richest fruit thus far of this effort of reading history in the interest of liberation.

The *theory of the theology of liberation* is still another of the varied accents within a single theology of liberation. Liberation is not blind praxis. It is in possession of a theory of its own, which gives it clear-sightedness and the capacity to confront difficult problems on the level of praxis and on the level of theoretical discussion.

There is a current within the theology of liberation that is concerned with theoretical questions. It deals with the epistemology of this new discourse on faith, with the correct articulation, or set of connections, between faith and social conflicts, or salvation and historical liberations, and with the methodological steps to be followed in order that theology of liberation really be theology. This endeavor provides the theological ''know-how'' by means of which one can do serious theology, defining problems and finding effective solutions. It is a sign of the autonomy of a stream of reflection when it can develop its own method and become aware of its scope and its limits. This point has now been reached by the theology of liberation. This confers credibility upon it vis-à-vis other ways of doing theology.

These are the principal tendencies within the one single theology that is surely the most fruitful one in the church today. On the eve of the Puebla Conference, all this theoretical and practical work began to be threatened by the atmosphere of tension, uneasiness—and yet, hope—that had been created, especially by the General Secretariat of CELAM. Would Puebla continue along the lines of Medellín, and thus extend the thrust of liberation? Or would it yield to fear and settle back into a spineless—or, at most, reformist—language?

The preparatory document, issued in January 1978, omitted the theme of liberation as the core and key of evangelization. Liberation appeared merely as one consideration among others in an approach to the social teaching of the church. There was vehement reaction the length and breadth of the continent.[16] The working document (August 1978) restored the concept and made it its central theme. Now the whole warp and woof of the text was shot through with liberation. Only an Appendix, devoted to the theology of liberation (synthesizing the apprehensions of the Ecuadorian and Mexican episcopates, with their conservative tendency) manifested an extreme inadequacy. But for the rest, the liberation perspective was solidly in place.

Then came Puebla. In the meantime, the atmosphere had changed in the universal church. Two popes had died, and a cardinal of the Second World had succeeded to the sovereign pontificate: Karol Wojtyla. Hopes caught fire.

Pope John Paul II's Liberation Thematic

Before entering upon an analysis of liberation in the Puebla Final Document, let us take time to reflect on the thematic of liberation as assimilated by Pope John Paul II, whose stance so influenced the course of deliberations at Puebla.

I note a certain evolution in his position. The pope moves from an attitude of reticence, even mistrust, to a surprising and enthusiastic support. His pilgrimage through Latin America did not leave him indifferent to the passion and suffering of workers, *campesinos,* and Amerindians. He came in contact with the reality that had constituted the original matrix of the theology of liberation. It can be said that, in general, the pope takes his distance from the vocabulary of the theology of liberation, but adopts its main theses.

But first we must give the lie to a report that appeared in the media, practically the world over. We were told that, even on the plane on his way to Latin America, the pope had been asked what he thought of liberation theology and that he had condemned it as a false theory. This is what the newspaper columns said.

Undeniably, the passions of the dominant classes, which control the media, and which had long since conceived a hostility for this type of theology on account of its criticism of their practices, was behind all this. In reality, what the pope had actually said was:

> Liberation theology, you know, is a genuine theology. But it can perhaps be a false theology. If theology begins to be politicized, begins to make use of systems or means of analysis that are not Christian, then it is no longer theology. Liberation theology, surely—but which?[17]

In the various discourses he pronounced in Latin America, the pope used the word "liberation" more than a score of times. His outlook is that of *Evangelii Nuntiandi* and adds little that is new to this apostolic exhortation. The accent falls on the integral perspective of liberation:

> That fuller liberation is "liberation from everything that oppresses human beings, but especially liberation from sin and the evil one, in the joy of knowing God and being known by him."[18]

Liberation, then, is preeminently religious; but because it is integral it includes socio-economic and cultural dimensions as well. The pope warns explicitly against reducing liberation to these dimensions.[19] He adopts the words of a catechetical lesson of Pope John Paul I:

> It is a mistake to state that political, economic, and social liberation coincide with salvation in Jesus Christ; that the *regnum Dei* is identified with the *regnum hominis.*[20]

Here it is important to understand the pope's meaning correctly, lest we have him contradicting himself. The pope rightly criticizes an identification that takes no account of the difference between salvation in Christ and historical liberation. He rules out a full and complete coextension between the upbuilding of justice and the kingdom of God. This would presuppose an identification of history with eschatology. On the other hand, the kingdom is indeed anticipated on earth, in history, and this is what happens with the upbuilding of justice. As Pope John Paul said to the workers of Jalisco, Mexico:

> Labor is a call from God to build a new world, one in which justice and a communion of brothers and sisters dwell—an *anticipation* of the kingdom of God, in which there will be neither defects nor limitations.[21]

In a nutshell, we could say: Liberation in Jesus Christ is not identified *with* political, economic, and social liberation, but it is historically identified *in* political, economic, and social liberation. I shall return to this in greater detail further on.

As I have said, the pope adopts the main perspectives of the theology of liberation. First of all, he manifests a profound sensitivity to the social drama of millions of Latin Americans. His first greeting on arriving in Santo Domingo was "to the poor, the peasants, the suffering, and the marginalized." At the Santo Domingo cathedral he came right out and denounced the situation of exploitation in which the rural and urban poor live—mistreated as they are and deprived of their rights—as "exploitation of human being by human being and by the state."

In his address to the Amerindians of Oaxaca and Chiapas, on January 28, he bluntly offered himself as "your voice, the voice of those who cannot speak or who have been silenced. [The pope] wishes to be the conscience of consciences, an invitation to action, to make up for lost time."[22]

"We must act promptly and thoroughly," he cried. "We must implement bold and thoroughly innovative transformation. Without further delay, we must undertake the urgently required reforms."[23] Returning to the idea of a social lien, or "mortgage," on private property,[24] he insisted:

> It is not just, it is not human, it is not Christian to continue certain situations that are clearly unjust. You must implement real, effective measures on the local, national, and international levels.[25]

In the face of this reality, the pope issued a call to action. There is a determined insistence here: the Christian inspiration for liberation should not issue from ideologies—he repeated to priests and religious—but from the gospel. The pope's position is that politics should be approached not politically but evangelically. The gospel cries for social involvement, for justice and liberation.[26] Christ himself is presented by the pope in his address to the bishops meeting at Puebla as having "outlined the model way of attending to *all* human needs," and as "identifying with the disinherited." His commitment was to the very neediest, the pope explains. "Christ did not remain indifferent in the face of this vast and demanding imperative of social morality," for these, too, pertain to the integral liberation he proclaimed.[27] Here we have the basic elements of a christology of liberation.

Pope John Paul II's first encyclical, *Redemptor Hominis*—which could be translated "Liberator of Humanity"—is pervaded by the perspective of liberation. The pope says very clearly:

> Today also, even after two thousand years, we see Christ as the one who brings man freedom based on truth, frees . . .

from what curtails, diminishes, and as it were breaks off this freedom at its root, in man's soul, . . . heart, and . . . conscience.[28]

The encyclical understands Christ's work within a framework of justice, that theme so dear to the theology of liberation:

The redemption of the world—this tremendous mystery of love in which creation is renewed—is, at its deepest root, the fullness of justice in a human heart—the heart of the first-born Son—in order that it may become justice in the hearts of many human beings.[29]

In his general audience of February 21, 1979, in Rome, Pope John Paul II declared to a large crowd of pilgrims from Italy and the world over:

The theology of liberation is very frequently associated—at times too exclusively—with Latin America. One of the great theologians of our day [Hans Urs von Balthasar] is correct when he calls for a liberation theology of universal dimensions. Only the contexts differ. The reality of the "liberty for which Christ freed us" (Gal. 5:1) is universal. The task of theology is to discover its authentic meaning in its various concrete, historical, and contemporary contexts.[30]

The pope goes on to emphasize that this subject "must be reincorporated into church teaching, in theology as in pastoral practice." This liberation means the human being's inward transformation as a result of knowing the truth." But this does not reduce it to that dimension. After declaring that "injustice, the exploitation of some human beings by others, the exploitation of the human being by the state, institutions, and mechanisms of economic systems, must be called by their name," Pope John Paul goes on to speak of liberation "on its many anthropological levels," and concludes that "liberation must be inserted into the entire contemporary reality of human life."[31]

The papal position is frankly positive. The pope recognizes that:

> Liberation is a faith reality, one of the basic biblical themes, deeply inscribed in the salvific mission of Christ, in the work of redemption, and in his teaching.[32]

The pontifical seal on this current of thought has showed a great deal of courage, in contrast to the attitude of those bishops who, at Puebla, did everything they could to obliterate the very name of theology of liberation.

Now let us see how the subject is treated in the Puebla Final Document.

The Puebla Liberation Thematic

Those who had hoped for a condemnation of the theology of liberation, or even for its silencing so that another theology could take its place, emerged from Puebla deeply frustrated. Puebla endorsed liberation theology and aroused an even deeper interest in it. Not only does it receive an ex professo treatment (part 2, chap. 2, no. 4) but it runs through the Final Document from one end to another like an axis. Liberation theology enters into the basic focus of evangelization in the present and future of Latin America: the creation of communion and participation via a process of integral liberation. The ultimate goal of all evangelization is to call forth a communion and participation of human beings among themselves and with God. Meanwhile, because communion and participation are not given, but have to be built, the process of liberation comes into the picture. The human being must be delivered *from* the impediments to communion and participation and *for* the concrete experience of communion and participation. "Our churches have something original and im-

portant to offer to all: their sense of salvation and liberation''
(Puebla 368).

The Final Document adopts, and everywhere reaps fruit from,
the established method of liberation theology: *seeing* (analysis of
reality), *judging* (judgment in the light of faith), and *acting* (determination of routes of pastoral action).[33] The point of departure
is a pastoral vision of Latin American reality. After considering
the historical, socio-cultural, and ecclesial dimensions of this
reality, and having taken account of the deep anguish and uncon-
querable hopes of Latin American peoples, the document draws a
conclusion:

> In a word, our people yearn for a full and *integral libera-
> tion,* one not confined to the realm of temporal existence. It
> extends beyond that to full communion with God and with
> one's brothers and sisters in eternity. And that communion
> is *already beginning* to be realized, however imperfectly, *in
> history* [Puebla 141; italics added].

From this seeing, there emerges a questioning, in order to
judge, in the light of faith:

> We now propose to proclaim the central truths of evangeli-
> zation: Christ, our hope, is in our midst . . . animating the
> church with his Spirit and offering his word and life to peo-
> ple today in order to lead them to full and complete libera-
> tion.
> The church, a mystery of communion . . . . Human be-
> ings, by virtue of their dignity as the image of God, merit a
> commitment from us in favor of their liberation and their
> total fulfillment in Christ Jesus [Puebla 166–69].

This is the reply of the Christian community to the question:
''What exactly is God's plan of salvation for Latin America?
What paths of liberation does God offer to us?'' (Puebla 163).

Acting follows from the dialectical relationship between the challenges of reality and the faith-reading that is made of those challenges. The whole remainder of the Final Document is concerned with rendering viable the paths the church must take to the realization of communion and participation.

The Final Document emphasizes, as never before in the history of the church magisterium, the social and political dimension of faith and of the evangelical message. The diagnosis is that we live in a situation of "social sinfulness" (Puebla 28), one "permanently violating the dignity of the person" (41). The remedy, then, must also be social: "Our social conduct is an integral part of our following of Christ" (476). And the document goes further:

So the church criticizes those who would restrict the scope of faith to personal or family life; who would exclude the professional, economic, social, and political orders as if sin, love, prayer, and pardon had no relevance in them [Puebla 515; cf. 824].

We read that the Christian attitude toward politics is a very positive one: "Far from despising political activity, the Christian faith values it and holds it in high esteem" (514); and "the need for the church's presence in the political arena flows from the very core of the Christian faith" (516). Politics, "in the broad sense" of seeking "the common good on both the national and international plane," with its "task . . . to spell out the fundamental values of every community . . . reconciling equality with freedom, public authority with the legitimate autonomy and participation of individual persons and groups . . . is a way of paying worship to the one and only God" (521; cf. 791). The dimension of liberation "belongs to the very core of . . . evangelization" (480), and is an integral, indispensable, and essential part of the very mission of the church (355, 476, 480, 562, 1254, 1283, 1302, etc.):

Manipulation of the church, always a risk in political life [is present when] priests and religious . . . proclaim a gospel devoid of economic, social, cultural, and political implications. In practice this mutilation comes down to a kind of complicity with the established order, however unwitting [558].

"Conversion" may not be conceptualized as something purely personal. It must extend to social transformation as well (362).

The Puebla terminology in this context connotes the abandonment of any hopes of merely reforming the system. The language of liberation implies something deeper. We hear of the need for "structural changes" (134), or "structural change" (1055), and a "transformation of structures" (438), which will reach the very bases of society (388, 438, 1055, 1196, 1250), indeed, which call for a new society (12, 642, 842, 1119, 1305).

The thematic of liberation receives an ex professo treatment in nos. 480–90 of the Final Document. Emphasis is placed on the importance of communicating to "the whole human being and all human beings . . . an especially vigorous message concerning liberation, framing it in terms of the overall plan of salvation" (Puebla 479).

What basic meaning is given to liberation by the Puebla document? From a great number of passages, it can be seen that the meaning is always that of *integral liberation*. This liberation is based upon "two complementary and inseparable elements . . . liberation *from* all the forms of bondage . . . [and] liberation *for* progressive growth in being" (Puebla 482; italics added). Integral liberation, as its name indicates, embraces all human dimensions: the personal, the social, the political, the economic, the cultural, the religious, "and all their interrelationships" (483). Again, in virtue of being precisely integral, this liberation will brook no reductionism—mutilation—that leaves out either "liberation from sin" or "dependence and the forms of bondage that violate basic rights that come from God" (485). Accordingly, it is a question of a liberation that "is gradually being realized in history" (483), and yet transcends that history (475).

All the activities of the Church should be permeated with the social dimension and liberation. Evangelization should be liberating (485, 487–88, 491). The liturgy is a privileged moment in this respect (895, 918). Christian education should explicitly proclaim Christ as liberator (1031). The church should present young persons with the image of Christ as integral liberator (1183). Prayer groups should be invited to become socially involved (958). All levels in the church, from hierarchy to basic communities (which are a motive force for liberation—96) should be the bearers of the message of integral liberation for all humankind and for the world.

Puebla recognizes that "the best service to our fellows is evangelization, which disposes them to fulfill themselves as children of God" (1145). It might be put this way: the mission of evangelization is summed up in liberating nonpersons and making them persons by delivering them from injustice, advancing human beings in all their dimensions (integral advancement), and, finally, divinizing human beings by bestowing upon them the full actuality of their status as daughters and sons of God.

The Puebla Final Document is also concerned with the problem that for us is the key one: the interrelationships among the different dimensions of liberation, especially between historical liberations and salvation in Jesus Christ. Here, says Puebla, with great perceptivity, lies "the great challenge" (Puebla 90, 774, 864), "the original imperative of this divine hour" (320): How can we be Christians, committed to our faith identity, and at the same time deeply committed to the liberation of our brothers and sisters? In the terms of the document, we must be armed with "a bold Christian profession and an effective promotion of human dignity" (320; cf. 511).

"Today Latin America . . . needs persons aware of their dignity and their historical responsibility. And it needs Christians [zealous for] their identity" (Puebla 864)—"builders," on the

one hand, "of a 'more just, humane, and habitable world . . .' "
(ibid., citing Pope John Paul II's homily in the Cathedral of
Santo Domingo, January 25, 1979), and on the other, builders
inspired by faith and the gospel. And so what is being asked for is
a vigorous, vital synthesis "between the faith they claim to profess and practice on the one hand, and the real-life involvement
they assume in society on the other hand" (783; cf. 320, 864),
between personal conversion and structural (economic, political,
and social) and mental changes (30, 159, 362, 438). Christians are
urged, then, to nurture a continuous personal conversion, cou-
pled with the simultaneous effort to achieve the transformation
of economic, social, political, and cultural structures.

For the Christian, historical liberation is not enough: the goal is
historical liberation from a point of departure in faith. Nor, on
the other hand, is simple faith enough for the Christian: faith
must manifest itself as a liberating faith, one that delivers other
persons from their servitudes. But faith there must surely be,
along with the religious practices (in the narrower sense) that
nourish faith (Puebla 142, 483, 796, 1225, 1253). Without faith,
Christian identity is empty and void.

Because it did not seize upon the opportunity to present a serious, substantial, and well articulated reflection on liberation in its
more theological, or theoretical, expression—an opportunity
that, in a way, cannot be recovered—the Puebla conference permitted certain ambiguities to creep into the Final Document.
Thus, for example, the conference calls for, and relies on, a
knowledge of theoretical and practical tools and means for the
transformation of society, in order "to shed light on the activity
of Christians if they are to avoid uncritical assimilation of ideologies on the one hand or a spirituality of evasion on the other"
(Puebla 826; cf. 85, 719, 1046, 1160, 1307). It is even recognized
that "ideologies seem to be necessary for social activity, insofar
as they are mediating factors leading to action" (535; cf. 539,
826).

On the other hand, the conference adopts an expression of
John Paul II that stands in need of clarification: "The church

'does not need to have recourse to ideological systems in order to love, defend, and collaborate in the liberation of the human being' " (Puebla 355—quoting the Opening Address of John Paul II at Puebla). There are many other instances in which the same idea is put forward—Puebla 119, 197, 213, 275, 276, 293, 416, 550, 551, 552, 693, 1113, 1145, 1153, 1194, 1221, 1309. This gives the impression that the church has everything and has nothing to learn (contrary to *Gaudium et Spes,* no. 40) and what is worse is the advocate par excellence of the process of the liberation of the peoples of Latin America.

This idealism, which wills the ends without willing the means and enunciates principles without concerning itself with their historical viability, could have been avoided by a better expression of the interrelationship between historical process and realization of God's kingdom, between socio-political liberation and salvation in Jesus Christ. It could have been shown how historical liberations are real mediations, however limited, of eschatological salvation—are anticipatory concretizations of the happy outcome of history, which God has already guaranteed in the victory of Jesus Christ.

Despite these limitations, I fully recognize the great contribution, surely on the mark, of Puebla in assimilating the liberation thematic and inserting it at the very heart of pastoral action and evangelization in Latin America. On the other hand, faith itself, in order to be genuine and salvific, may not be allowed to remain indifferent to the "cry . . . rising to heaven, growing louder and more alarming all the time. It is a cry of a suffering people who demand justice, freedom, and respect for the basic rights of human beings and peoples" (Puebla 87; cf. 24, 28). *How can we be Christians in a world of peoples in misery? We can do this only by means of a liberating faith.* This demand was perfectly well heard and articulated by Puebla.

The Puebla Final Document manifests, then, extreme sensitivity to the liberation *thematic.* But the same cannot be said with regard to the *theology* of liberation, which seeks to be a systematic reflection on praxes of liberation. A minimal expression of praise for this theology, present in the penultimate redaction of the Puebla Document, was expurgated under pressure from bishops more concerned about caution than about offering any incentive for original theological reflection—which is of course ever the victim of narrow horizons.

This fear of theological reflection in a framework of liberation had the effect of a mighty curb in the doctrinal part of the material on evangelization—the "content": "The Truth about Jesus Christ . . . the Church . . . Human Beings" (part 2, chap. 1). The typical Latin American theological reflection is missing—a step-by-step consideration of how Jesus Christ, by his works, his message, his committed life, and his courageous death effectuated liberation, in a historical and transcendent time. Just the other way about, the document presents the dogmatic teaching on Jesus Christ, and the faithful are asked to "accept this liberating teaching" (Puebla 180). It is as if it were not Jesus' teaching that is liberating, but rather the teaching of the church about Jesus that becomes liberating.

The same thing is to be said about the section on the church. Insufficient effort was made to gather together the ecclesial experiences of recent years in Latin America, experiences lived under the sign of participation, communion, and liberation, and to draw forth from these experiences the ecclesiology latent within them. A doctrine of the church is presented that in many points is more rigid than that of Vatican II.[34]

But it is especially in the doctrinal part of the document that the effort of theological reflection on the horizon of liberation is lacking. In the other parts of the document, it is theology that serves, and is subordinate to, the great pastoral themes, as has been shown above. There the theology of liberation appears as it seeks to be understood—as a theology practiced at the heart of pastoral praxes, with a view to a living synthesis of faith with socio-historical reality. It is in this perspective that the document encourages Latin American Christians "to explore the particularly conflict-ridden situations of our peoples in terms of the faith and to shed the light of God's word on them" (Puebla 470; cf.

376, 479, 687, 806, 1240). Still, there are warnings about possible ambiguities (178, 342, 375, 628, 676, 990) and risks, particularly in the use of any Marxist tool for the analysis of social reality (544–46).

Resituating the Key Problem of Liberation Theology

In this section I should like to present a critical repositing, and repositioning, of the crucial problem of the theology of liberation. It is time to reevaluate the foundational perspective of that theology and to make an efficacious effort to find the correct approach to the articulation of a rigorously theological discourse on liberation.

Value and Limits of a Global Theological Discourse: Integral Liberation

The global theological discourse expressed in the terminology of integral liberation maintains a legitimate value to the extent that it expresses the eschatological and utopic perspective of the Christian faith that underlies a total liberation at the term of history, with the emergence of the full freedom of the children of God. The utopic element pertains to reality and elucidates all the potentialities residing in history that are fully realizable only in transhistory. Meanwhile, this transhistorical element exercises a historical function: that of constantly nourishing hopes for an absolute future anticipated in our intrahistorical futures—the latter actualizing values that are relatively closer to what is utopic. Indeed it has the function of relativizing all concrete historical liberations and of keeping our perspective open to the future and the transcendent. In this sense the utopic furnishes criteria for an ethical critique and adjudication of the various historical concretions of liberation.

The limitations of this utopic discourse appear when it comes time to concretize it in a reflection on the socio-historical mediations that might produce genuine anticipations and approximations of the utopic. Here the necessity of a pertinent "regional discourse" is imposed—one that will speak of concrete historical realities. We now descend from the sphere of the utopic and enter that of particular determinations. And it is here that the discourse on integral liberation manifests its intrinsic limitations. It runs the risk of "dehistoricizing"—of evaporating in pure phraseology, in words without substance. Indeed it is easily susceptible of ideological utilization, precisely in virtue of its universalizing, vague nature. Whenever anyone points to historical liberations on the economic and political level, we hear at once: "Be careful; liberation is integral and involves spiritual liberation from sin."

This approach runs the risk of depriving concrete discourse on the economic and political level and on the anticipation of the kingdom (which can indeed be present in these instances) of their respective substance. That a liberation not be the eschatological kingdom does not prevent it from being the kingdom in anticipation. One cannot do everything at once—nor is this what the gradual upbuilding in history of the eschatological kingdom demands. One might as well say, with regard to some liberation of the heart from deviant and sinful attitudes, "Be careful; liberation is integral—it has to include liberation of the economic infrastructure, and political and cultural elements, as well as a liberation of the heart."

As is evident, then, the expression "integral liberation" lends itself to interpretation now in one sense and now in another; thereby depriving concrete historical liberations of their density, their substance, their genuineness and legitimacy.

I believe that this type of theology of liberation, as a vision permitting a synthesis of the whole historical process understood as a dialectical process of oppression and liberation, and thus covering all dimensions of personal and social life, is complete and adequate. It furnishes conceptualization capable of serving as point of departure for the development of a broad, comprehensive vision of the Christian mystery—as a mystery of the liberation of humankind and the world *from* the captivities to which they are subject and *for* ever fuller forms of life, communion, and participation, culminating in God and the kingdom of God. Indeed, this approach in itself presents no shocking novelty. The Christian faith has always maintained this vision. As Pope John Paul II said so well, in the address in which he pronounced his encomium of the theology of liberation, on February 21, 1979: "This theme of liberation has never ceased to constitute the content of Christians' spiritual life." It is only that it has "come within a new historical context."

Return to the Original Discourse: The Theological Element in Socio-economic Liberation

The real novelty of liberation theology consists in the development of a rigorous discourse on the theological element present in socio-economic liberations. Accordingly, it must take up a "regional" theological discourse—it must limit itself to a single, clearly circumscribed "region" of reality, the socio-economic. It has no concern, at this stage, for a universalizing conception of liberation. It attends to a historical process of liberation, within which a faith understanding endeavors to discern a theological dimension. Let us address this problem with all care and exactness.

A process of liberation is underway, being carried on by the subordinate classes. This liberation is economic, political, social, and pedagogical. The people, a poor people, is organizing, facing up to the strategies of domination of the hegemonic classes. Subordinate classes are succeeding in reinforcing their power and thus establishing more equitable relationships among the various social forces. This process is being carried out principally at the economic and political levels, with repercussions on the ideological and pedagogical. It involves struggles for a more symmetrical and more just social configuration. It entails commitment and involvement at times maintained to the point of the sacrifice of one's security, employment, and even life. A certain dignity attaches to political engagement for universal causes such as the defense of human rights, especially those of the least favored, the struggle of organized labor against deteriorating living conditions, and other causes arising from directly historical situations and orientated toward changing these situations.

There are, in this engagement, this task, this struggle, a great many Christians who find inspiration, encouragement, and enlightenment in their faith. It is their faith that enables them to struggle, to commit themselves to their sisters and brothers, and to participate in liberating processes.[35] Liberation, then, is no mere idea. It is a historical reality.

Now the question of central interest to us is posed. How is this liberation, already underway, related to God, to the kingdom, to the salvation brought by Jesus, to grace? Socio-economic liberation is transformed into material for theological reflection. The liberation in question is not an integral liberation. It is this precise historical liberation. What does reflective Christian faith— theology—have to say about it? How do committed Christians make this material the subject of their prayer, their encounter with God, and perhaps indeed their rigorous and serious reflection (theology)? Can they say that here, in precisely this historical reality, they are in the service of the building of God's kingdom? If the answer is yes, then how do such Christians actually know that they, by participating in this socio-economic liberation, are building the kingdom of God? Where does the light come from? How does one know? As is evident, an adequate explanation is imperative.

Classic theology theologized on overtly theological material. It reflected on God, Jesus, sin, grace, heaven, and the like. These themes are theological *in recto*. These subjects do not need to be constructed. They are given by religion. But now a new need arises. A theological discourse is to be developed on materials that are not theological *in recto*—that is, they are not presented as theological. They are secular—economics, politics, education. These fields have their own discourse. There is political science discourse, pedagogical discourse, and economic discourse. How may such material, in itself secular, be transformed into theological material? The theological element is not given; it has to be constructed. How may the theological element present in economic and political material be constructed?

This is the key question. This is the real challenge for a theology of liberation. In other words: How may we see the presence of God, and God's grace—or the presence of the evil one, and sin—within economic and social processes?

Classic theology has not reflected systematically upon this question. It has posed it, but it has not developed a grammar that might have exempted us from the toil of creating one. It is in the effort to respond to these questions that the novelty and creativity of a so-called theology of regional liberation will have the opportunity to come to expression.

How a Theological Discourse May Be Assembled on Economic, Political, and Social Elements of Reality

The question now is how to extract the theological dimension (the salvific dimension, the divine signification) present in socio-economic realities from such realities themselves, so that it may "inform"—permeate and give meaning to—and illuminate the praxes of committed Christians.

Here there is a certain precondition to be defined. We must identify the social locus from which theologians interrogate social reality, along with the three basic mediations by which they do so. First it is imperative to have a pertinent knowledge of the material in which one claims to discover the presence of the theological element. This knowledge is acquired by socio-analytic mediation. Secondly, one must read the theological element inserted into economic, political, and social material—and this is done by hermeneutic mediation. Finally comes the task of determining the efficacious practices that flow from what has gone before—the praxis sprung from faith-articulated-with-social-analysis, the activities that will be of assistance in the process of the liberation of the oppressed. And this is the theoretical mediation of practice.

The rigorous "grammar" of this manner of discourse has been

detailed in the important work by Clodovis Boff, *Teologia e prática: Teologia do político e suas mediações.*[36] As Adolfe Gesché, professor of systematic theology at the University of Louvain, writes in the Preface:

> No theologian, even if working in other areas of theology, can dispense with this book. . . . The author has truly written a discourse upon method thanks to which a theology can truly be pursued in these domains and can rightfully be called theology.[37]

But now let us address the question posed above: how to assemble a theological discourse upon socio-historical realities.

Antecedent Political, Ethical, and Evangelical Option: for the Poor and against Poverty.   Unless it is to evaporate in metaphors and euphemisms, a theology of liberation requires of theologians a clear definition and consciousness of their social locus.[38] Any theology whatever has a social place, a position. A theology is always socially situated.

The theologian of liberation opts to see social reality from a point of departure in the reality of the poor—opts to analyze processes in the interests of the poor, and to act for liberation in concert with the poor. This is a *political* decision, for it defines the theologian as a social agent, occupying a determined place in a correlation of social forces: a place on the side of the poor and oppressed. At the same time it is an *ethical* option, because it rejects the status quo. It refuses to accept the situation as it is and experiences ethical indignation at the scandal of poverty and exploitation. It evinces an interest in the advancement of the poor, which can occur only in the presence of structural change in historico-social reality. Finally, it is an *evangelical* definition: in the gospels, the poor are the primary addressees of Jesus' message and constitute the eschatological criterion by which the salvation or perdition of every human being is determined (Matt. 25: 35–46).

Socio-Analytical Mediation.   Once the basic option has been defined, the next stage of the process of liberation theology is the construction of a correct analysis of social reality. The option for the poor is of itself no guarantee of the quality of this analysis. The latter must be carried out by some instrumentality that can bring to light the mechanisms generative of poverty and the paths that lead to liberation.

It is of the utmost importance to clear away certain basic epistemological obstacles that present an *a priori* impediment to a correct grasp of social reality.[39] The first obstacle is *empiricism*. Empiricism describes the facts but fails to establish any causal nexus among them. What is lacking is analysis.

A second obstacle resides in *theologism*. Theologism expects to be able to explain all problems, even political ones, and furnish all solutions, in terms of theology. The legitimacy and contributions of other discourses are not acknowledged. Theology is substituted for social analysis.

Thirdly, there is the epistemological obstacle that I call *bilingualism*. Analysis and theological reflection can be simply juxtaposed, yielding two readings of reality without mutual articulation. What is yielded here, then, is what I call "unarticulated analysis," or "inarticulate analysis."

Finally comes *semantic commixture*. The same two languages are simply mixed together, by drawing now on the resources of social analysis, now on those of theology. The result is a conceptual hodgepodge, to the detriment of both analysis and theology. What is left is an ill-fashioned articulation of the two.

Once our analytic gaze has been purified by the elimination of these three epistemological impediments, we are prepared to come to the task of social analysis. Here we must either make our own analysis, or adopt the analyses that social scientists have already made. Which analysis is to be preferred? Which social theory is to be adopted?

Here the determination of our social place, our social locus, comes into play, and we must ask ourselves why we are making our analysis at all. We are making our analysis with a view to the liberation of the oppressed. Now, two basic tendencies prevail in social analysis: the functionalist, which sees society by and large as an organic whole; and the dialectical, which sees it in a special way as a complexus of forces in tension and conflict by reason of the divergency of their interests.

It seems to me that the dialectical analysis better answers to the concerns of the poor and the powerless. Functionalist analysis is reformist. It is concerned with the functioning and improvement of a system it judges to be good, one that it thinks ought to be maintained. Dialectical analysis examines conflicts and imbalances affecting the impoverished and calls for a reformulation of the social system itself, in order to secure symmetry in the system and justice for all its members.

This is why the theology of liberation opts for the dialectical analysis of social reality. Liberation theology holds that this is the analysis that better answers to the objectives of faith and Christian practice. And it is here that use is made of the analytical instrument devised by Marxist tradition (by Marx himself, by the various contributions of socialism, by Gramsci, Althusser, and other theoreticians). The utilization that liberation theology makes of this instrument is not servile. Dialectical analysis is science, divorced from its philosophical presuppositions, divorced from dialectical materialism. Science is knowledge submitted to control by experimentation and verification. Philosophy is a universalizing interpretation of being and global history. It is Marxist science, and only science, that will serve our purposes.

In the analysis of social reality in the dialectical approach, the data of social anthropology and social psychology, along with considerations of history, also come into play. Everything must conspire toward a structural and causal comprehension of the situation of poverty in which millions of Latin Americans live, a situation that, within an ethical framework, must be considered inhumane and unjust.

Hermeneutic Mediation. Now we come to the next "moment" in the epistemological process of liberation theology: that of the theological reading of social reality, as now critically deciphered by analysis. The theological reading of reality is a reading in the light of faith. This secular material must be transformed into theological material.[40]

How is this procedure to be implemented? An epistemological rupture must be introduced here, a change of focus: the theologian is now interested in knowing whether God, God's grace and salvation, are or are not present in some particular reality that has been critically analyzed. If the answer is yes, the theologian must further determine in what form this divine dimension occurs there. Accordingly, reality is now read from another perspective—another relevancy, or *ratio formalis*. The "reading glass" is furnished by Christian faith.

A like "reading" presupposes, in the interest of the hermeneutic mediation itself, philosophical reflection. Philosophy poses the question of the whole of the real. That is to say, a social analysis covers only one segment of reality. But human reality is more than its social aspect. It is personal, as well; then it opens out upon other sectors, other segments, of reality; and finally, it is capable of striking a relationship with the Infinite. All this makes up the human being's concrete reality.

Accordingly, social analysis must take account of its limits. It must be antidogmatic. And it must take account of its regional character, and respect other views of reality.

This philosophizing consideration is decisive for theology, given the ultimate and totalizing nature of theological key concepts (God, revelation, the offer of salvation, Christ's universal redemption, and so on). God is present in the social, to be sure—but God's presence and activity are not reduced to the social area. They are not confined to this single region. God penetrates, permeates, all aspects of reality. And so the discourse on integral liberation, a process of total liberation, as we have already observed, secures its legitimacy.

But our particular interest centers on the presence or absence of God in this one region of reality: the area of the social, the economic, and the political. What "reading glass" does theology use to discern God in this reality? We are dealing with an authentic theoretical praxis here, a practice by means of which knowledge is produced. We have raw material (social reality as deciphered analytically), to which we apply theoretical instruments (theological categories), in order to extract a theological product (the theological reading of social reality). Let us list the key categories by means of which we read secular social reality theologically.

The first category of our theological reading is *faith*. Faith is the existential attitude that interprets all reality from a point of departure in God—in the Christian determination, from a point of departure in the incarnate God, Jesus Christ. By faith, one seeks out and deciphers an absolute meaning—a meaning of meanings—in reality, one that will embrace the whole of that reality, including the economic, the political, and the social. By faith one sees all things as ordered to God or deviating from God. All things fall under the *dispensation of salvation or perdition*.

The order of salvation and perdition is the only concrete order we have. It is the only order that de facto exists. It is by reference to this order, then, that all human good, all justice, all fellowship, all grace and salvation—and all evil, all injustice, all oppression of one human being by another or of human beings by the state, all sin and perdition—exist. From this conceptualization it is then deduced that economic, political, social, and pedagogical material, in the light of faith, "always has an objective, or structural, soteriological significance—independent of the social agent's knowledge or intent."[41]

As synonymous pairs of correlates with salvation/perdition, we can also contradistinguish salvation history and perdition history, the kingdom of God and the kingdom of this world, and grace and sin.

Explicit faith raises one's consciousness—conscientizes a person—with respect to the objective salvation/perdition that become and are reality even without anyone's consciousness of it. Salvation/perdition are appropriated, assimilated to oneself, via (good or evil) *moral practice,* even in the absence of any awareness of one's orientation to salvation or perdition.

Theology is simply faith in quest of understanding. It is the cry of faith, transformed into the grammar of a rigorous, structured discourse—whether it be discourse on immediately given theological material such as God, salvation, grace, and the like, or discourse on realities in which a reference to salvation/perdition is not overt but is nonetheless objectively present, as is the case with the positive or negative salvific value of economic mechanisms, political strategies, or social structures.

To put it in simpler language: Christian consciousness maintains that, from the first beginnings of history to its final term, God always has and always will offer salvation to all human beings. Consequently, "the ultimate vocation of man is in fact one, and divine" (*Gaudium et Spes,* no. 22).[42] In this perspective, there are never two histories, one secular and "natural" and the other sacred and "supernatural." The only real history, in the concrete order of things—which could have been different (hence the importance of the theological *concept* of "pure nature")—is the history of salvation/perdition. All is contained, bounded, by this dispensation—all human behavior and all dimensions of life, personal, social, political, economic, and so on. Accordingly, in this perspective, there is a theological component present in all the material with which we are concerned—the economic, the political, and the social.

Salvation history is not to be confused with *revelation history*—the history of the explicitation of this salvation. Revelation is posterior to salvation, and the vehicles of the former are only certain persons, not all—even though revelation is addressed to all. Salvation—which is offered to all, and is appropriated by all through their respective moral praxis, independent of any reflexive awareness on the part of the agent of moral praxis that salvation or perdition is linked with that praxis—tends to come to consciousness, to become explicit, to transform itself into a discourse (the discourse of explicit faith, of theology), into a liturgy, into a code of conduct. Biblical revelation is the official explicitation, elicited by God (through inspiration, and endorsed in canonicity) of this intrinsic tendency of the material salvation process to become formal and explicit. The church is the organized "space" of this salvation consciousness—the event that celebrates salvation, and the institution that organizes salvation consciousness in communitarian fashion.

In biblical terms, it can be said that the kingdom of God comprises all realities, human and cosmic: they are all destined to constitute the object of God's lordship and the glory of God's *operatio ad extra* (all of God's activity other than intratrinitarian). Everything in existence, then, pertains to the kingdom. Economics, politics, and society all possess an objective "theological density."

The incarnation of the eternal Son of God in Jesus Christ possesses a supereminent heuristic significance: God the Son has assumed unto himself the totality of human life, including its infrastructural dimensions—its biological, economic, social, personal, religious moments, and so on. Everything that exists, therefore, is "sanctifiable." Everything is a potential sacrament of the presence of God in history—even economic, political, and social material. This material is what it is, to be sure. But it is also part of the incarnation of God the Son. It therefore has a potential holiness, which must be enunciated by the discourse of faith.

Further, a correct understanding of eschatology accords theological value to this material. The eschatological defines the final status of the human being and of the world in God. But it views that status as indeed the *final* status, as the ultimate outcome of a penultimate moment—as the result of a historical process that begins here and now and culminates in eternity. As Vatican II says: "On this earth that kingdom is already present in mystery. When the Lord returns, it will be brought to full flower" (*Gaudium et Spes,* no. 39).[43]

These categories of faith, as grasped by and set forth in the scriptures, afford the possibility of an *interpretation* (and this is why I say that they pertain to the "hermeneutic" mediation) of the justice or the injustice of a given social configuration as the presence of salvation or perdition, the presence of the kingdom of God or of the antikingdom, the presence of grace or of sin. Faith adds nothing to the social configuration *ontologically:* it sees, within that configuration, its *theological moment,* and explicitates it theologically. This is what I mean by a faith reading of social reality interpreted analytically.

Mediation of Pastoral Practice. The socio-analytical reading of reality, articulated by the hermeneutic reading of this reality in the light of faith, should lead to pastoral practices of transformation.[44] These praxes, springing as they do from faith and always marked by the consciousness of faith, will impinge upon a social reality that stands in need of transformation in the direction of the ideals that faith constructs, and indeed transform it in the direction of these ideals—of social justice, human dignity, and a community of participation in everything by all. A critical knowledge of reality determines the paths to be followed by faith on its way to efficacy. The goal is genuine liberation: hence it is crucial to achieve a verifiable effectiveness.

Here certain criteria are to be observed. First come the criteria of *faith* itself. The inspiration of a given praxis must be evangelical. The motive for an action must spring from the matrix of faith itself. Faith, of its very nature, and the church, as the organized space of the faith experience, are located on the symbolical level of message—the level of impulse to personal conversion—and on the level of the praxes that fall within the ambit of pastoral theory and action.

In the second place, there are criteria to be observed that emerge from *reality.* One must attend to the correlation of forces at work and make prudential judgments as to what is feasible, what is permissible, what is viable—and all of these under what conditions. On this level it is important to consider what forces one may rely on for auspicious alliances, as well as what manner of reaction may be expected on the part of those who wield power, along with their allies in the global system.

Those Christians are to be respected who, under the inspiration of faith, develop functional ideologies of transformation and organize transforming praxes, without thereby seeking to involve the whole faith community as such. Here there is an open space for action that cannot be taken by the institution, but that nourishes the life of Christians who, for their part, although reared by the institution, undertake commitments for change that the institution itself and as such may not be able actively to participate in, although it may comprehend them and so be able to lend the support of faith and understanding.

All these steps constitute inseparable moments in a single theological process of understanding and efficacy—a process concerned with historico-social realities in which, here too, human salvation or perdition is at stake.

Articulation between Salvation in Jesus and Historical Liberations

It should be clear from what has been said thus far that, for Christian faith, "salvation" is a technical term, expressing the eschatological condition of the human being, risen and divinized, in the plenitude of the kingdom of God in eternity. But this definitive situation does not spring up full-blown only at the term of history. This situation is anticipated, prepared for, within the historical process. On the one hand this salvation totally surpasses the historical process and is thereby "transhistorical." On the other hand it is within the historical process that this salvation is situated. And because it is situated within the historical process, we may speak of a theological element present in economic, political, and social material. When the church, for example, concerns itself with politics, it does not do so *politically,* struggling for power with other competitors. It does so *theologically:* it discerns, within political material, a dimension of salvation or perdition—a theological dimension, then, that is accessible only to the understanding of faith, not to that of political science.

The kingdom, although not of this world in its origin—it comes from God—is nevertheless among us, manifesting itself in processes of liberation. Liberation is the act of gradually delivering reality from the various captivities to which it is historically subject and which run counter to God's historical project—which is the upbuilding of the kingdom, a kingdom in which everything is orientated to God, penetrated by God's presence, and glorified, on the cosmic level as on the personal level (the level of divinization). Liberations show forth the activity of eschatological salvation by anticipation, as the leaven of today in the dough of a reality fully to be transfigured in the eschaton.

Let us now return to an earlier question. How is this eschatological salvation related to historical liberations? In other words, what is the nexus between integral liberation and partial liberations (liberations on the economic, political, and social levels)?

But before taking up this problem itself, it will be in order to deal with a problem of an epistemological nature: the meaning of analytical and theological languages and the nature of the distinct dimensions of one and the same reality that each language apprehends and translates.

We must begin with the fact that, once more, there are not two histories and two realities. There is one only. Still, this single, self-identical reality possesses a plurality of distinct objective dimensions. Each of these objective dimensions can be grasped apart from the others; hence the various species of scientific discourse, each with its proper viewpoint, its own concern, its "formal object." These distinct discourses do not create corresponding realities, corresponding things, but translate distinct dimensions of one and the same reality.

Analytical language, for example, speaks of a society of exploitation or a society of cooperation, or of unjust structures, or of mechanisms of domination, or the like. Religious language, reading the reality thus analytically deciphered, perceives that the analytical dimension has reference to a deeper dimension, one in which this reality touches God: faith discerns in injustice the presence of sin, and in mechanisms of exploitation the presence of social sin.

It is important to keep in mind that there are not two realities here, though there are plural dimensions of one and the same reality. We must not conclude, from the fact that faith speaks of a kingdom of God or an antikingdom, and not of a just and symmetrical society, that the kingdom or antikingdom have nothing to do with a just or unjust society. The kingdom takes flesh in justice—though it is not simply synonymous with a just society, for it is also realized in dimensions other than the social. Kingdom of God and just society are not totally coextensive. But they overlap. Hence we can speak of an identification of the one *in* the other, though not of an identity of the one *with* the other.

What, then, is their relationship?

I shall present four models of articulation between them: the Chalcedonian, the sacramental, the agapic, and the anthropological. Each of these models of articulation will involve both oneness and distinction—*identification* without total *identity*.

Chalcedonian Model.   The supreme example of how salvation and liberation are interrelated is given to us in the personage of Jesus Christ. In him is revealed both God's salvation and human liberation—the unity between God's design and its historical mediations.

The Christian faith regarding Jesus Christ, as formulated by the Council of Chalcedon in the year 451, professes that one and the same Jesus Christ, without confusion, without change, without division, and without separation, is at once "God and man" (DS 302).[45] The union obtains "saving the properties of each of the two natures" (DS 293; cf. 302, 509, 555). Jesus Christ is from two natures, and he subsists in two natures (*ex duabus et in duabus naturis*—DS 302; cf. 414, 506, 555, 2529), but these two natures are so unified that they constitute *one and the same Jesus Christ*.

In christological terms, to speak of Jesus as God in such a way as to imply that he is not human is monophysitism—the heresy that attributed only the divine nature to Jesus. To speak of him as a human being in such a way as to imply that he is not God is Nestorianism—the heresy named for Nestorius, which asserted Jesus' humanity to the point of negating his divinity.

Humanity and divinity in Jesus are interrelated in such a way as to constitute a "unity in duality." Nor is this mutual relationship without its tensions, for on the one hand we have a creature, a human being, and on the other hand the Creator, God. These two beings are on different ontological levels. And yet they are related in such a way that the human Jesus can say, "The Father and I are one," or, "Whoever has seen me has seen the Father" (John 10:30, 14:9). In the incarnation, not only is God transcendent and a human being immanent: both have become "transparent," in virtue of the presence of the one in the other. On grounds of the incarnation, then, we can say that this concrete humanity includes God, and God includes the human being. But because the properties of each remain intact, we must also say that this human being, Jesus, is indissolubly conjoined to God, yet remains ever an immanent human being; and God, although hypostatically conjoined to this human being, radically transcends him, remaining ever the transcendent God who dwells in inaccessible light.

This schema has a heuristic meaning for the problem of the salvation-liberation relationship. Salvation and liberation are distinct; but they are united, without confusion and without separation. It is monophysitic to assert that there can be salvation without historical liberations; it is Nestorian to assert that there can be historical liberations without an openness to salvation.

To put it in other terms, salvation intrinsically includes historical liberations. Jesus, our salvation, is also our liberator: he conjoins salvation to liberation. Deeds and praxes not in themselves religious—healing, restoring sight to the blind, and so on—are presented as concrete forms of the presence of the kingdom of God (see Luke 7:21; Matt. 12:28). At the same time, salvation transcends every historical liberation, for death has not yet been vanquished: we have not yet come within God, nor have we been totally assumed by God, nor has all creation been transfigured.

Thus, just as there is only one Christ, so also there is only numerically one history of salvation/perdition. Historical liberations are God's salvation by anticipation, God's salvation taking place inchoatively. Historical oppressions are perdition, proclaimed in advance along the way of this human pilgrimage. For the Christian, heaven does not come only after this earthly life. It is already within this earthly life. But it is not in its plenitude here. It crosses out beyond, it transcends, this life, to touch eternity.

Christian experience does indeed attest to a duality, but not to two things juxtaposed. It attests to two moments in a single process, each of them present *within* the other. Eschatological salvation comes by way of historical liberations. No one is introduced to salvation by magic, but only through effort for and commitment to the liberations that anticipate and prepare definitive salvation.

Salvation and liberation are without division and without separation, but they are also without confusion and without any change of one into the other. By reason of sin, liberation is never full and complete: it always carries a quota of oppression. Salvation is total liberation, and thereby it is salvation fully achieved—completely unsullied and pure, never again to be threatened. In Jesus' words, the kingdom is now near (Luke 10:9), it is in our midst (Luke 17:21), it already exists (Matt. 4:17); and at the same time it is future and the object of our supplication (Luke 11:2; Matt. 6:10, 19:28).

Sacramental Model. We understand "sacrament" here in its original sense of *mysterium*.[46] In this sense, a sacrament is "a visible deed of God, by means of which the divine salvific will is signified and rendered present in the historical dimension of human beings."[47]

In this acceptation of the word, all grace and salvation possess a sacramental structure. Grace does not come like a beam from above. It is offered us "mediatized," offered us as a sacrament: as mediated by some wordly reality to which it is united. The great prototype of this sacramentality is sketched out in the incarnation of the eternal Son of God. He is sacrament at its source, the Sacrament in which the human and divine are found definitively unified. The church in its totality, and the seven sacraments of the church, constitute special concentrations of this sacramental principle, which in turn characterizes all grace and salvation history. Historical events are charged with grace or sin. Events are sacraments.

The tragedies of history result from the fact that sacramental structuration permits a cleft, a hiatus. History is not always the vehicle of salvation. Salvation is not indissolubly conjoined to this or that historical sign or reality. Realities can communicate ungrace: they can be the vessels not only of weal, but of woe.

This does not mean that grace fails to find some other incarnational path in such an instance. Grace always comes in sacramental form—that is, mediated by the socio-historically visible. But no reality in itself, apart from Jesus Christ, is exclusively and indefectibly a sacrament of grace. This means that grace is always found united to a mediation, but that it is always free vis-à-vis *this* or *that* mediation.

Because grace is sacramentalized but never fixed, the importance of the distinction between temporal growth and salvation is clear. Not everything commonly considered to be progress anticipates the kingdom of God. There is a growth and development that originates in selfishness, in concupiscence, in the will to power—in a word, growth can be the expression of sin. This is not the kingdom, but the antikingdom. Accordingly, in order to enter into the kingdom and live in grace, conversion is needed—opposition to the undertakings of "this world" (in the Johannine sense). Such conversion can entail persecution (Mark 10:30) and a share in the lot of the Son of Man. Meanwhile, whatever actualizes justice also strengthens love and opens the human being to God and to the presence of the reality of the kingdom being concretized within the limits of space and time.

Justice is justice and love is love, to be sure. They can be the object of rational analysis. But for faith they are a sacramental presence—within the dimension of history—of the grace of God. *This* justice and *that* love cannot claim to be the whole of justice and the whole of love, because they are historical and limited. But to the extent that they are genuine love and genuine justice, they are messianic realities and the material of the kingdom of God. In historical time, in a situation constituted *sub regimine peccati*, no socio-historical concretization is of such unalloyed purity as to constitute the only sacramentalization of grace. Only in the definitive eschatological kingdom will the world, and the human beings who have been saved, be the transparent sacrament of God and of God's love. Until then we live in mutually compenetrating symbolical (unificative) and diabolical (divisive) dimensions. Accordingly, there will be liberations in process that will not be totally identified with definitive salvation. Sacramentality is fragile: it can shatter. There can be such a thing as growth that is ordered to perdition, not to salvation. Consequently it will not be a sacrament, anticipating the kingdom of God in history and rendering it visible.

What is important to retain is that just as in a sacrament grace is always conjoined to a sign, and never appears as grace *simpliciter*, so also historical liberation is always conjoined to salvation—even though salvation is not present in historical liberations alone, just as grace can be had independent of any *particular* sign.

Agapic Model.　　The New Testament, and Jesus' teaching especially, give us to understand that one who has love has all things (Matt. 22:34–40; cf. Rom. 13:9–10). One who loves God and neighbor—commandments having the same value (Matt. 22:39)—possesses life simply and absolutely (Luke 10:25, 28). In Saint John it is clear that God is love (John 4:8, 16), and that whoever loves their brothers and sisters loves God (1 John 4:20–21). In the parable of the last judgment Jesus is not only in solidarity with the "least ones," he is identified with them ("You did it for me . . . you neglected to do it for me"—Matt. 25:40, 45).

The "lowly" are the "unknown God." Love of God and love of neighbor are identified—an identification so profound, so deep, that God and salvation are actually found in the love of one's neighbor, especially when the neighbor who is loved belongs to the oppressed, of whom the parable of the last judgment speaks. God is sacramentally present in a unique way in the oppressed human being—without prejudice to God's transcendence, of course, for God overflows human reality.

The root of this identification is to be found in the Holy Trinity. Every human being is daughter or son of God in the eternal Son: he or she is eternally thought and loved in the eternal, incarnate Son. And so there is something divine in a human being, just as really and genuinely as love for another person implies and involves love of God.

There is, then, a unity and a distinction: love for the created person continues to be human love, with all its historical concreteness; but simultaneously that same love is love for God, who is present incognito in the depths of every human being—as well as within love itself, for God is love (John 4:8, 16). In human love there is an ontologically divine dimension—that is, a theological dimension. Historically, the eternal Son, in whom we are God's offspring (Eph. 2:10), became incarnate as the suffering Servant. Hence all the sufferers of history are special sacraments of Jesus Christ, the suffering Servant. In them we find a deeper and more concentrated presence of Christ.

The intimate relationship between love of God and love of neighbor helps us to understand the intimate relationship between salvation and liberation. Neither is purely synonymous with the other. But each is present in the other, in such a way that they are always together, and can no more be separated than confused.

Anthropological Model.   The concrete human being is a unity-in-duality. Body and soul should not be understood as two *things* making up the one human being. Body and soul are two concrete *principles*, together forming a single thing, the human individual. Principles are not things. They are what enable us to understand things—in this case, body and soul are the principles that enable us to understand the concrete human being in its unity-in-duality. The Vatican II expression is excellent: "Though made of body and soul, man is one" (*Gaudium et Spes*, no. 14).[48]

We might say that the body is the whole human being understood as a being turned toward earth—a historico-social being that partakes of the limitations and the mortality of all other created beings. We might say that the soul is this same whole human being turned toward heaven—capable of transcending all limitations and projecting itself into the Infinite that is God. The concrete human being is the coexistence of these two dimensions, the immanent and the transcendent, within one another—unified with each other, but disproportionate. Spirit is totally within the body, but it is not buried with the body: it transcends the body, and can strike a relationship with the totality of beings and with God.

The anthropological model—which shows the oneness and distinction, the duality within one and the same being, the human being—gives a key to understanding the oneness and the distinction subsisting between eschatological salvation and historical liberation. In historical liberation (corresponding to the body in our model) is the whole of salvation (corresponding to spirit); but this salvation is no more shaped by the confines of a historical liberation than spirit is shaped by body. Salvation always transcends liberation, just as spirit transcends body. Without coinciding totally, then, salvation and historical liberation nonetheless constitute the unity-in-duality of one single history—just as body and spirit constitute the dual unity of the human being.

The relationship between eschatological salvation and historical liberation, despite the light that these noetic models can shed on it, preserves, withal, the character of mystery. This relationship cannot be totally grasped by thought.

The various approaches outlined here all demonstrate the intimate relationship (the identification) of salvation and liberation, but they also reveal their differentiation (their nonidentity). This is the tension that constitutes the dynamic of a history moving ahead toward the kingdom of God.

Liberation Theology and Faith Experience

My approach to the basic problem of the theology of liberation—namely, to identify the theological element in secular realities such as socio-historical liberations—neither despoils nor ideologizes faith in its transcendence, in its face turned toward the totality of God's salvation. It answers to the demand that faith be more concrete, the demand that faith be effective, and that it transmit its efficacy to the oppressed.

In Latin America, nearly all the oppressed are Christian. The faith that these Christians live is not an adornment, extrinsic to their afflictions. It is the motive force for liberation here and now, for the historical translation of the salvific deed of Jesus Christ and the salvific will of his Father.

This theology grounds a spirituality of commitment and of encounter with God and Jesus, in the struggle for the transformation of the world into one more worthy of the human being and more like the new world of the kingdom of God.

In order for the liberation effort to preserve its theological identity, it must be able to elaborate an adequate discourse. The theology of liberation (in its "regional" sense) has at its disposition a "grammar" by means of which rules are established for this new field of reflection on the faith, together with the correct diction for a foundational discourse.

But the correctness of theological discourse is not enough. This discourse must express, in articulate fashion, a faith experience, a contemplative, mystical vision of socio-historical realities. It is not enough to say that there exists within these realities an objective dimension of salvation/perdition. Theology also has the duty of *actualizing* this dimension on the level of this faith experience. But this is possible only if this faith experience exists. And it exists only if the space of faith is created and nurtured in ongoing fashion by prayer, meditation on the scriptures, and, finally, by Christian praxis. This praxis interiorizes the faith dimension, thereby creating the "eyes" by which we discern that, in socio-historical realities, the kingdom of God is realized or frustrated, here on earth.

Every star, a certain philosopher used to say, has need of the atmosphere in order to shine. Just so, all theology of liberation has need of nourishment in the atmosphere of a mystique, a spirituality, in order to maintain its vitality. A genuine commitment to the political, and to liberation processes, demands of believers special moments of prayer—moments of the explicitation of their faith experience.

It is here that our Christian identity is created—from which point of departure our passion for God, for God's kingdom and justice, is transformed into a passion for the poor and oppressed, with whom we enter into solidarity, and with whom we identify. Then the liberation produced will be an authentic anticipation of definitive salvation, and those who produce it by their effort and striving will be authentic artisans of the kingdom of God.

3

CLODOVIS BOFF

Society and the Kingdom: A Dialogue between a Theologian, a Christian Activist, and a Parish Priest

The Liberation Problematic

Theologian. Puebla adopted the vocabulary and thematic of liberation once and for all. What a step this was, in the area of theory, along the path our Latin American church is treading! An irreversible step, a point of no return. Medellín had already broached the liberation thematic. But it was just a beginning. No further development was guaranteed—until the 1974 Synod of Bishops brought the same problematic under discussion, and with such vigor. Then the results of the synod were gathered together in *Evangelii Nuntiandi*, in 1975. Now the language of liberation flowed smooth and sure. The signal had been given. All that was left for Puebla to do was to *consecrate* the language of liberation, along the lines of *Evangelii Nuntiandi*. It didn't consecrate the so-called theology of liberation. And it would have had no business in doing so. But Puebla collected its most expressive results, setting up some solid framework for further developing that theology. From now on, Latin American theology can carry its task forward with more courage. Not that Puebla solved all the problems: in fact it raised some new ones. Here too Puebla was just a starting point, and we are still working out its ramifications.

So let's get to work. We're going to have to discuss this whole liberation problematic. It's as if it were challenging us to see if we know what to say about it. Shall we start by defining what we mean by liberation?

Rhetoric of Liberation

Activist. For me, liberation isn't a figure of speech or "image" of some kind. Liberation is just plain liberation. It's the poor getting out of their situation of oppression. Sure, it's a whole process, and it'll take time. But when I say "liberation" I mean something concrete. I mean this: get the system of injustice over with, get capitalism over with. Get free from it, to create a new society in its place—say, a socialist society.

Priest. I've nothing against that—only, the liberation the church preaches is an "integral liberation," a complete one, a liberation of the whole person and every person. Reducing liberation to a purely historical process is what I call "horizontalism." Christian liberation isn't just the political emancipation of a people. Something has to be added to that: the most important thing, the religious, the spiritual, the supernatural dimension. Just read the Puebla conclusions carefully. It's clearly stated that Christian liberation has to be integral, complete—personal and social, in this life and in the next: liberation *from* slavery, liberation *for* communion.

Activist. That's nice. It's easy to talk that way. Everything seems solved. Everything seems clear and sure. But the question is: How do we arrive at this integral liberation? The raw fact is there: the great majority of our people are suffering hunger. They're living in humiliation. They're living in conditions unworthy of human beings. How can you talk about the liberation of the "whole person" when persons are being crushed in a situation like this? It looks as if you want everything all at once.

Priest. For Puebla, liberation has various dimensions. One is the political dimension.

Theologian. The question here is to see how the different dimensions of liberation are interrelated. Puebla just made a statement, that's all. It didn't go any further. If we are satisfied just with statements, we fall into a *rhetoric of liberation*. We hear endless disquisitions on liberation—that it has a human dimension and a divine dimension, that there is liberation "from" and liberation "for," and so on and so on.

In all this talk, in language like this, words shift around as they please. Puebla even says in some passages that liberation is a dimension of evangelization, of faith, of the church. But many persons are thinking of historical, political liberation—in other words, commitment to social transformation. In this sense, liberation coincides with rescuing the people from their slavery. In other places, Puebla turns it around: faith and evangelization are dimensions of liberation, because liberation has to be integral—so it has to be religious, too, spiritual, not just political. Here, then, liberation covers what we usually call salvation, redemption, grace.

So some are wondering: Is liberation a quality of faith or is faith a quality of liberation? But notice, in the first case "liberation" is being used as a sociological term, and in the second case it's being used as a theological term. In the first case, liberation is a historical reality: it's the people uniting, organizing, and mobilizing to defeat misery, oppression, and alienation. In the second case liberation is a metaphor for the mystery of salvation, just as "redemption" is a metaphor: the buying-back of slaves so they can go free.

In this religious rhetoric it's easy to slide from one level to another, and you don't notice differences in language. Now it's sociology talking political liberation, and now it's theology talking liberation in Jesus Christ. This language-mix goes by the nickname of "semantic hash." This type of discourse can be brilliant, as any rhetorical discourse can, but will it shed any light? I'm afraid it obscures more than it clarifies.

Levels of Liberation?

Priest.   But even theologians, even the best-known ones—Gutiérrez, Assmann, and others—make distinctions among the various levels of liberation. For instance, they state that there's a social level, a cultural level, and a spiritual level too.

Theologian.   True. They've always talked about integral liberation. And they've sorted out the different levels. This was a good thing in the beginning; it got discussion going. But at the present stage of our pastoral and theological journey, this sorting-out of various levels of liberation has been seen to have a basic theoretical flaw. Today it presents problems—the kind of problems called "aporias," because they're posed in such a way that there can't be any solution.

We might formulate these aporias this way. Is integral liberation, on its various levels, a homogeneous continuum? For instance, do we get liberation of the heart, and then it goes on to social liberation, and then social liberation leads to its furthest limit? Shouldn't the relationship be different? Shouldn't we say instead that each of the levels of liberation is implied in the other, by a kind of mutual inclusion?

You can see from these questions that lining up the various levels of liberation in a list is not very satisfactory theologically. It's not the way to set up the question. This is "extrinsicism," and extrinsicism is a sign of theoretical weakness, not to say theological misery.

Priest.   But today everybody talks the way Puebla talked. The questions you're raising are the concerns of particular little groups that seem to like to complicate the question rather than explain it.

Theologian. Surely, Puebla's language is a pretty good reflection of the way liberation is talked about in our countries. But theological research has now established certain basic principles for speaking correctly and logically about liberation in the light of faith. What we're dealing with here is the "epistemology" of the theology of liberation. These principles can no longer be ignored today. This would be just prolonging the use of a language that shows that it's "confusionist"—which makes it ideological, because it *covers problems up.* It's like continuing to do astrology after astronomy was invented, or alchemy after chemistry was founded.

Activist. What's epistemology?

Theologian. The study of knowledge. It's so you can reflect correctly. In the case of theology, epistemology is seeing how you can construct a serious theology. Take the theology of liberation. What we have to do is examine the requirements for making the theology of liberation a theology and not something else. To keep talking a *religious rhetoric of liberation* when we now have a *theological theory of liberation* will no longer do, and some of us can't stand it any more.

The first liberation theology—a theology that never existed before in history—the first liberation theology came to us mixed with social science. It had to. But then it was hard to know just what we had—sociological theology or theological sociology. One young activist caricatured it this way: "Liberation theology? Poor man's Marxism."

Now, it seems to me, it's time to get beyond our "theological oedipal stage." It's time for the "epistemological break," and the inauguration of a new discourse, a free discourse. This is the first "liberation of liberation theology" that has to be accomplished. The objective conditions, theoretical and practical, for the emancipation of a theology that studies liberation are already present. If this theology starts out with a correct, proper epistemological assent of the mind, it can strike up a mature dialogue with the social sciences. It'll be learning a new lesson, and teaching one. Those who resist a "theological oedipal break" will run the risk of becoming "religious ideologists of liberation," and others will see that that's what they are. Of course, we'll have to be patient— we have psychiatry now, but we still have fortune-tellers too!

Priest.   But bishops don't have to do theology. They're pastors. Their job is to encourage communities along their path. They're not supposed to invent theological theories.

Theologian.   Without a doubt. But liberation rhetoric is becoming worrisome. It no longer satisfies certain more demanding persons in the church, either in theory or in practice. It sets up roadblocks, including pastoral roadblocks. Therefore it would be in the interest of the bishops themselves to improve their language, their basic theology underlying their pastoral discourse. After all, they all have a theology, consciously or not.

"Metaphor Mania": What Is Liberation?

Activist.   I'd like to go into this a bit. From what you're saying, this is what I see: when we hear about "liberation," there are always some who understand it to mean liberation from sin, spiritual liberation— and then maybe eventually liberation from suffering—relief, consolation, as a kind of spin-off. This is the bad part. These persons, whenever they hear anybody say "integral liberation," right away start thinking of heaven. Material liberation doesn't count, because material misery doesn't bother them. What interests them in the question of "integral liberation" is the spiritual side—interior liberation of the soul.

If it were only the soul they were really talking about! Most of the time they just *think* they are. Liberation of the heart for them doesn't mean conversion; it doesn't mean a change in personal values. It doesn't mean a change inside and outside. It's more of a change of feelings, a change in their way of looking at things, and that's where they stop. To my way of thinking, this is spiritualism, pure and simple.

Priest. But you can't reduce everything to the material, or the social. The human being is more complex than that. Persons have their anguish, they have dramas going on inside them. There are a great number of persons in our countries who are in despair. They're looking for a meaning in life without using faith, without loving anybody. There are many who are *spiritually* poor, and they're worse off morally than those who are materially poor.

Activist. There it is, right there. No sooner do you start talking poverty than you start thinking "spiritual" poverty. Material poverty? There's no such thing! Or if there is, it's not worth bothering about.

And the same thing happens with other words. For instance all you have to do is say "basic community" and you've got those who think "basic community" means a little group of do-gooders getting together for dialogue, mutual aid, and so on. There's never any question of the poor, of the masses, of the ones at the bottom of society, the oppressed majority.

Theologian. This way of treating words—just stuffing them with a spiritualistic content—is what I call "metaphorizing." It's not just a mannerism, it's a mania. Words don't have their common meaning any more—their real, material meaning. They only have a metaphorical sense, a figurative one, a symbolical one. This is what happens with words like "poverty," or "basic," or "oppression," and so on. This is a kind of "language kidnapping." "Metaphorizing" is a kind of sublimation of language. You don't change the words, you change the semantic content, and you throw them on the market in that condition. You kidnap a whole vocabulary, and force it to speak in a metaphorical key. This way you can distract attention from concrete reality. You pretend the reality of material poverty isn't there, you pretend social oppression and liberation processes just aren't going on. Metaphorizing "dematerializes" all this, makes it "nonreal," as if it didn't exist, or at least didn't deserve much attention.

Activist. Look, this "metaphorizing"—if I get your

drift—is pretty much all "flour out of the same sack," as we say. You can see, it's always upper-class persons doing it. Misery, hunger, and oppression don't mean anything to them. For them this sort of thing is always somebody else's problem.

Therapy for Theological Language

Theologian.   You've hit the nail on the head. That's why I say liberation vocabulary is sick, and we've got to find a cure for it.

Activist.   But that can't solve a thing. Those who spiritualize words do so because of the way they live. They do it because they're all set up, they're comfortable. For them there's no point in grabbing hold of things as they are. They can't stand to look reality right in the face, look at it stark naked. Why should they? Then they'd have the accusing finger pointed at *them*! They'd have to quit thinking that poverty is the problem of the poor. It's *their* problem, because they're the ones who cause poverty and keep it going. Then they pretend they don't see anything, so they won't have to "get involved." And the worst part is, all this goes on more or less unconsciously.

The same thing happens with liberation. If the comfortable classes were willing to face up to reality, they'd see that what's at stake in the people's struggle for concrete liberation is *them*. And they don't want to see that! So they try to distract their attention and everybody else's from the present reality of poverty and the future possibility of catastrophe. That's the way I see it.

So you can forget about curing liberation language, as far as I'm concerned. The privileged classes are the ones who need curing. The basic problem is not liberation language, it's liberation. When the people is liberated, *then* theology can be liberated from all these "sublimations," as you call them.

Theologian.   But you still haven't got hold of the whole thing. Theology mustn't wait for a liberation in the future in order to start to work. True, it can only help. Liberation is a whole process, and theology has only one role in it. But it does have a role. A theological problem isn't going to be solved by political liberation. That's why if we make an effort to apply good therapy to theological language, we can contribute to the solution of the big problem—the people's liberation. I admit that this theological task doesn't dispense us from political struggle. But it can help in the struggle by shedding light on it. And this is truest of all for Christian activists.

Activist. Well, I can't fault that. If a cured, healthy theology can work for liberation instead of muddling things up, so much the better.

Theologian. And I'm looking ahead. You see, until now we've been satisfied with a pragmatic, or "instrumentalist," view of theology. Our supreme interest has been social liberation, and we've focused theology in the light of liberation. Or you can turn the problem around this way: *What* liberation are we talking about? Now it's theology calling the shots and liberation that had better look alive. I find that this is the way that Christians pose the question of social liberation. A non-Christian activist—a Marxist, for instance—will never pose the problem in these terms. As far as theology or religion is concerned, a non-Christian activist will at most try to make use of them, and stop there.

Christian activists can stop there too. But in this case they have missed the specifically Christian aspect of the question, which is: What is the faith meaning of liberation? What does faith have to say about the struggle for emancipation? In what sense, and under what conditions, does this struggle actualize the kingdom of God? It's not going to be just *any* liberation that will do it. There are liberations that lead only to a worse slavery. There are purely nominal liberations, just as today we have lots of "revolutions" with nothing revolutionary about them but the name. The liberation a Christian is after is the one that accords with the gospel ideals of justice, peace, and a community of brothers and sisters. In other words, the liberation a Christian is looking for is one that realizes, in history, the transhistorical notion of the kingdom of God.

Does Kingdom of God = Classless Society?

Priest.   Exactly. The kingdom of God is not simply a classless society. It is infinitely above that. Salvation is not simply political liberation. It is something else, an infinitely superior something. Salvation is not in the same order of things as liberation. Salvation isn't just a deeper and deeper and more radical liberation to the point that you finally get salvation. They're not the same *sort* of reality. Salvation is transcendent. There is no proportion between salvation and liberation. Salvation is a divine, supernatural work. Liberation is a political, historical, work.

Activist.   How do you define "salvation"?

Priest.   By salvation I understand redemption, reconciliation, grace, the kingdom of God. All these expressions refer to the same transcendent reality. Salvation belongs to the order of mystery, and no words can define it adequately. That's why many words are used, in order to be able to say at least something about it. The image of the kingdom of God is one of the most powerful images for suggesting the marvel of this genuinely supernatural reality. And this was the image Jesus used. In a nutshell, salvation means the total, absolute actualization of the human being.

Activist.   That's not how I define it. To me all this is very abstract. It's hard to understand. To me, the kingdom of God that Jesus talked about is a society of brothers and sisters, a just and free society. Look: salvation is liberation. It's having done with the misery the people suffers. And sin—sin isn't something purely spiritual, something just on the inside. It's exploitation, it's injustice, it's oppression, it's chains on persons in this world, external chains, that destroy them. Conversion is a change of structures, and in this sense it's revolution. All these words— kingdom of God, salvation, sin, conversion—these are all names that Christians have for concrete, natural, historical realities— fellowship, liberation, oppression, social transformation. It's a question of words. The things are the same. One person uses religious words, another uses secular words, but both are actually saying the same thing.

Priest.   No doubt about it. But I'm not defending a purely symbolic liberation. I'm not even defending a purely spiritual liberation. I'm only saying that historical liberation isn't everything.

Activist.   But then what's this spiritual liberation of yours, this "spiritual dimension" that's tacked onto historical liberation?

Priest.   Grace. Liberation from sin for communion with God our Father.

Theologian.   But what does "spiritual" really mean? If we think the way the ancient Greeks did, "spiritual" means "pertaining to the human being's spirit." It's a synonym for a person's inner self, a person's inner being. If this is the meaning, then "spiritual" is the opposite of "material," or "bodily." But if we think the way the Bible does, "spiritual" means "pertaining to the Spirit of God," the Holy Spirit. This Spirit of God is not opposed to matter, to body, to the human being, to the world. On the contrary, the Holy Spirit is embedded in matter. The Holy Spirit animates the human body, dwells in the depths of a person, fills the world. The Holy Spirit is the opposite only of nonbeing—death, or evil: injustice, destruction, domination, contempt, unlove . . . sin.

Activist.   If that's the way it is, spiritual liberation isn't liberation of the soul. It's liberation of the person—a liberation under the impulse of the Spirit of God. Even political liberation can be inspired by the Spirit of God, by the power of God. It was that way with the exodus. That was a "spiritual" liberation too, then, in the biblical meaning of "spiritual."

Theologian.   Right. So everything that is done "according to the Holy Spirit" is "spiritual"—even when people are dealing with material things, like eating and drinking, working, having children and raising them, loving, feeding the hungry, clothing the naked, and today, struggling for and with the oppressed.

Activist.   The Holy Spirit is in *this* world, not some other world. Grace and sin are things in our history: justice and injustice, liberation and oppression. And that's it.

Priest.　　They're that too, but not only that. All oppression is sin, but not all sin is oppression. So also all liberation is grace, but not all grace is liberation, at least not in the political sense of liberation.

Activist.　　I don't have anything against that. Only, for me liberation is liberation, period, and that's it.

Theologian.　　Here we have to understand one another. We have a problem of expression here—a question of language.

Activist.　　I still think the problem is a lot more basic. When you come right down to it, it's a matter of different, contrary social positions.

"Language of Materialization"

Theologian.　　I'm not ruling that out. Only, it seems to me that before we get into any other approach, we have to deal with a question of language—a question of understanding one another as to the words we're using here. We'd better handle this question first. Otherwise we'd be trying to solve a theological problem with a sociological explanation. After all, it seems to me, it's just as much a mistake to metaphoricize a reality as to reify—make a thing out of—a metaphor. Strictly speaking, we ought to say: it's as erroneous to make a metaphor out of a *concept* whose content is material, sociological, as it is to materialize a *metaphor* whose content is spiritual, theological. Or we could say it this way: whether we theologize sociology or sociologize theology, we're off on the wrong track.

Priest.　　How about a little explanation of what you mean by "materializing a metaphor."

Theologian.　　I'm talking about a certain perversion, a certain twisting, of language, and here's how it works. It takes a metaphor, like "kingdom of God," for example, and understands it according to its literal, material, immediate content.

"Kingdom of God" then becomes some society (a real or a possible society) that is in fact a reconciling, just, and good society. "Kingdom of God" would be a kingdom of human beings, insofar as it were to be a social system of brothers and sisters living in freedom. It would be a classless society, you might say.

Activist. And what's wrong with that?

Theologian. To my way of thinking, this would be to make a divine concept a worldly one. It would mean degrading the notion of transcendence. It would mean lowering the notion of the kingdom of heaven to the level of a particular historical concretion.

Activist. That's the error of "horizontalism," or "immanentism." That's politicizing the kingdom of God.

Theologian. Here we're talking about a *manner of understanding the divine.* We're not even talking about a way of *dealing concretely* with the divine. God is above all our manipulations. God is strictly inaccessible to human effort. God never permits a "self-profanation," a reduction to the level of the worldly. What *can* be "profaned" is an *idea* of God, a representation of God, or even a manner of access to God—a religion. But God is above all our efforts at horizontalism, politicization, or use as an ideological tool.

Priest. What is the correct way of understanding the idea of the kingdom of God, then?

Theologian. In its essence, the kingdom of God that Jesus talks about is not any society that politics speaks of. So also, the salvation a Christian talks about is never in itself any liberation that a Marxist talks about. Society is a matter of the historical, the objective, the relatively manipulable. The kingdom isn't. The kingdom is transhistorical, it's a divine gift, a mystery—if you like, it's a "nonobjectivizable" reality. You can never say about the kingdom, "Here it is," or "There it is over there," or that it'll come today, or tomorrow, or this way or that way. This is the way the gospel thinks of the kingdom.

This is something we have to be very clear on. Society is a profound, complex reality. Society as a sociologist studies it is not society as lived by men and women in their total experience. Sociologists grasp only one dimension of society. Theologians, for their part, grasp another dimension of society. But it is not simply another dimension, it is a deeper, a more global dimension than that caught by the sociologist. Of course, both the sociologist and the theologian are speaking of one and the same thing—society; only, each perceives it in a deeper or less deep dimension, each according to their own perspective or interest.

And so there is no contradiction between the sociologist's view and that of the theologian. There's an articulation, a nexus, a set of connections, between them. Obviously, the theological, divine, salvific dimension of society is not going to be of the same nature as the sociological dimension. This has to be kept in mind, because today's culture has a tendency to reduce society to its social aspect. It is as if society were only what social analysts see and explain. If that were the way things are, there would be no point whatever in constructing a theology of society, unless by "theology of society" you meant the purest of religious fantasies.

Activist.   But the kingdom of God has to be in this world. Where else would it be?

Theologian.   Right. But we're getting ahead of ourselves. Right now I'm only trying to define the kingdom of God itself. Only afterward can we say, "The kingdom is in this world." If we don't know just what the kingdom of God is, we can't very well say it's in this world.

Activist.   But how do we get to that point—I mean, how do we get an idea of what the kingdom of God is itself?

Theologian.   By taking the concept of an ideal society, perfectly reconciled, and with that as a launch pad making a leap: the leap of "transignification." Transignification is a semantic operation consisting in opening an image up to the infinite and attributing to it an infinite degree of significative power. It means the extreme maximalization of its "evocative force." It means taking the image out beyond all bounds of relativity.

Activist.   For me, the kingdom of God is just a religious name for the ideal society. To whatever extent we improve society, by perfecting its organizational form, we are approaching the kingdom of God.

Theologian.   The kingdom of God is not simply a utopia situated on the horizon of history. It is a reality already present at the heart of history. And it is present even where there is oppression, to whatever extent a struggle is underway to overcome that oppression.

Activist.   A classless society is a better expression of the kingdom of God, then, than a class society.

Priest.   If you head off in that direction, you'll have to say that communist societies that have actually abolished social classes are a better expression of the kingdom of God than are Christian societies where classes still exist. And you'll have it said that there are institutions that are better "sacraments of salvation" than is the church!

Theologian.   Here we have to make a distinction between a historical or social expression of the kingdom of God and a sacramental expression of that kingdom properly so called. But let's let that go. The important thing is to take the expression "kingdom of God" for what it is: it's a metaphor—a metaphor for a transcendent reality, which is the divine salvation of human beings.

It's the same with the word "liberation." We must take it for what it is: a *concept*—the concept of a historical reality, the reality of the social emancipation of the oppressed.

This is not the place to discuss the truth of religious metaphors—whether they say only something about human beings (that they're fooled, or alienated, as many critical theories of religion say today), or whether they really say something about God (that God is transcendent, mysterious, as theology presupposes). But the only way we can correctly articulate the relationship between these two terms—the metaphor and the concept—will be to get them correctly defined.

Language of Identification: "Topical Realization"

Activist. Salvation and liberation are two things that always go together.

Theologian. They go together in concrete reality, but they don't go together in your head. They're not the same concept. And it's the head's job to find the thread running through the tangle of yarn that is complex reality.

Priest. Well, how are you going to find the "thread" running through all this tangle?

Theologian. By starting out with the following datum of faith: the kingdom of God has come. It's among us, in this world. Therefore the kingdom is within our society. It's inserted, incarnated, in society, in history, in the world. Not that the kingdom is *identical with* the world. The kingdom is *not* purely and simply the world. But it is *identifiable in* the world. This is where we find it. So we have to avoid a pure and simple *language of identity*—the kingdom is the world—and adopt the language of what I call *topical realization,* or *"installation":* the kingdom is *in* the world. After all, as Saint John says, "The word became *flesh* and made his dwelling *among us"* (John 1:14).

It would not be correct to say, then: salvation *is* liberation (or vice versa). The correct way would be: salvation is (installed) *in* liberation (and vice versa). In this way it is not a language of *identity pure and simple* or *identification with,* but the language of *identification in,* the language of "topical realization."

Priest. "Topical realization . . . ."

Theologian. Yes, meaning that the kingdom is realized here in society. This is its locus or place of expression, its *topos.*

Priest. But society isn't the only place or *topos* of the expression of the kingdom. The kingdom is also realized in the depths of us, in each of our hearts—for example, when there's a conversion, when a person opens up to God in faith and hope, in adoration. The kingdom is realized in interpersonal relationships—when persons love one another, pardon one another, accept one another. And the kingdom is realized, too, in a *topos* that's not a *topos* at all—life beyond death, in the *"topos"* we call heaven. It's there, especially, that the kingdom finds its place of maximal realization, its *pleroma,* meaning its fullness or completeness, its *parousia,* meaning its definitive presence and epiphany, its triumph and its glory!

Theologian. Nothing could be more true! Society is but one of so many *topoi* of the realization of the kingdom. Of course it's not the only place—though today it does turn out to be the main place. This is why we say that society constitutes a "topical realization" of the kingdom, and not its "realization *simpliciter.*"

We could say the same thing in different words: the kingdom is *identified in* such or such a society—a just society of brothers and sisters—but is not *identified with* it. That is to say: the kingdom shows in society, it is encountered in society; but this society is not simply the kingdom. The kingdom and society do not completely overlap. This will happen only in the parousia, Christ's second coming, when God will be all in all, and the kingdom will be whole in all society.

Society: Chrysalis or Theater of God's Kingdom?

Activist. To say that society is the "place" where the kingdom happens—I find that this still isn't enough. It's not only the stage, the setting, the scenery, where a people's destiny is played out. It's not like setting up a factory, where you're interested only in factory operations and what the factory will produce. It's got to be more than that.

Theologian. The precise modality of the relationship between salvation and liberation is not easy to grasp. The relationship exists—but *how* does it exist? What is it like? As far as I'm concerned, we have to begin by admitting that this relationship is somehow divine, and hence mysterious. Listen to this from Vatican II: "On this earth that kingdom is already present in mystery."[49]

If this is a presence in mystery, then, it can be understood only through analogies, figures, symbols. There is no precise word or concept for grasping the kingdom-society relationship, the salvation-liberation relationship. We use analogies to say something about it; then we multiply those analogies, in order to be able to seize more and more of its profound, immense, infinite reality. Each of our figures tells us something about this relationship—gives us a new perspective. No analogy exhausts its meaning, not even all our analogies together. But one says something another cannot. So the analogies we use all have a somewhat different meaning.

Priest.   Can you give us some examples?

Theologian.   For example, Dubarle calls society the chrysalis, the cocoon of the kingdom. Nikolai Berdyaev says practically the same thing: the kingdom is the *noumenon* of human history—its ultimate essence. Along the same lines, but using a different type of analogy, Saint Augustine uses the figure of pregnancy: he says history is "pregnant with Christ"—*historia gravida Christi.* It's as if the kingdom would be the whole Christ himself, gestated in the womb of the history of human beings—Christ taking on historical form. So too we say that the *theotokos,* the virgin mother of God, is a prototype of salvation history.

Vatican II, in the same passage I mentioned before, also says: "here grows the body of a new human family."[50] We have the use of the word "body." And the same document says that the Holy Spirit calls certain persons "to dedicate themselves to the earthly service of men and to make ready the material of the celestial realm."[51] So we have another image: "material." Then the council recalls the eucharistic mystery, which we have for so long described in terms of "transubstantiation," calling it "that sacrament of faith where natural elements refined by man are changed into his glorified Body and Blood."[52] This parallelism of the political activity of liberation with the sacrament of the eucharist is profoundly suggestive. Finally, the council uses the biblical figure of "new heavens and a new earth" (Rev. 21:1), showing once more that the "other" world, the kingdom, is not distinct from this present world, but substantially identical with it—only, renewed and transfigured.[53]

Activist. All these images show a very strong relationship between salvation and liberation, between the kingdom and history. I think we could actually speak of an "incarnation" of the kingdom in history.

Theologian. And there you have still another figure: "incarnation."

But we also find, in biblical and theological texts, another whole series of figures that see this same relationship not along lines of identity—topical identity—but along the lines of the *difference* between the two terms. Vatican II, in the same passages already mentioned, along with the biblical images I mentioned, speaks in other figures too. For instance, there is the image of a "shape."[54] This is the word the council uses to translate Saint Paul's word *schema,* in 1 Corinthians 7:21: the "shape of the world," or "the world as we know it," which is surely "passing away," and the council cites this passage to this effect.[55] The council is talking about the regimen, the dispensation, the order of this world. The Bible says the same thing using the word *aion,* "age," *saeculum.* This order, this dispensation, this age, must pass away.

The fathers of the church used the expression "economy" or "disposition." What they were saying is that this historical logic of ours, with its class struggles, contradictions, and phenomenon of domination—this "nature," which we know today to be rigidly governed by the laws of thermodynamics in a cooling universe—this sweep of the evolution of life, which is a struggle for life in a world of the "survival of the fittest," of so-called natural selection—and so on—this type of thing, this "logic," all this is to be done away with.

The council also uses the image of a "foreshadowing": human society "even now is able to give some kind of foreshadowing of the new age."[56] This world would be only a sketch, then, a kind of first draft, a model, a sample, of the kingdom.

Saint Augustine, in putting our history in perspective with God's history, uses the image of a scaffold: He says: "The [divine] architect builds, with temporary structures, a lasting edifice."[57] Bruno of Solages has another suggestive image. He says that civilizations are "shipyards of the kingdom of God." And we could go on and on.

Priest.   This time all the images put a heavy accent on the relationship of difference, of exteriority, between the kingdom and history.

Theologian.   Yes. Each of our images has something true to say about the relationship. It would be a mistake to use one without the other, or one series to the exclusion of the other. And this raises an important question, especially where our praxis, either pastoral or political, is concerned. What line of images should we prefer? Which one should we emphasize? The identity or the difference? The theater or the chrysalis?

Activist.   The chrysalis. To my way of thinking, we have to accentuate the idea of intimate union but not identity. The general tendency among Christians today is to distinguish the kingdom and this world too much—to separate them from one another. The danger today is dualism. Even the council took note of this,[58] and Medellín emphasized it even more. Then Puebla was strongest of all. For Puebla, a separation between faith and the reality of injustice is a contradiction, a tragedy. Puebla says that this is the great historical challenge to the Latin American church.

Priest.   Puebla also insisted that committed Christians must not lose their Christian originality. They must always be aware of their difference.

Theologian.   I find that the primary accent should fall on the intimate oneness between salvation and liberation. And then, as occasion arises, the distinction can also be pointed out.

Activist.   Here's how I'd do it. Four times out of five I'd put the stress on the sameness, and the rest of the time on the difference. The main point would be, "the reign of God is already in your midst" (Luke 17:21).

Priest.   For Marxists, or Christian activists, I'd emphasize the difference. For them, I'd say, "The kingdom of God is not of this world." They make social change the absolute imperative. A new society, the classless society, is for them the ne plus ultra of history, the eschatological *pleroma . . ., the millennium! To me, this is sheer utopia.

Activist. But the big temptation for Christians today happens to be dualism. They think of God as outside the world. Faith can't be separated from the world. A kingdom of God separate from the world, all ready and waiting—that's a fetish! And a fetish is alienating. God and God's kingdom are always incarnate in history.

Priest. Faith can also find itself alienated in some of its forms. Not just any incarnation of faith is good.

Theologian. Faith can have many "objectivizations." There are *alienating* ones—the ones where faith is "denatured" and lost. This is when religion becomes a foreign force, and turns against the human being. So when religion is used as a cover for racism, sexism, domination, exploitation—those are alienating objectivizations. Ideological manipulation of religion is another example.

But there are *authentic* objectivizations of faith, too. Faith is expressed in concrete liberating acts, and the paradigm for all of these cases is in the parable of the good Samaritan.

But faith has to become incarnate. There's no doubt about that. Faith contains, within itself, an openness, an intimate need, to "take flesh." Faith becomes genuine only when it real-izes this "constitutive tendency" it carries deep within it.

Ethical Bond between Salvation and Liberation

Priest. Well, it's obvious there's a relationship between salvation and liberation, then. And another thing we've said is that this relationship is sui generis—that it's of the nature of a mystery, and that therefore it can be grasped only in an inadequate manner, that is, by analogies or metaphors. We also agree that the understanding of this relationship can vary, all the way from a vision of profound identity, to an immense difference between the two terms of the relationship. Finally, we realize that salvation is not always given, is not always positively realized, in history. Now we need to analyze in what conditions it is given, in what conditions it is positively realized in history.

Theologian.   The cord that lashes salvation to liberation is, first of all, the salvific will of God. God has willed it so. God has determined it to be this way. As far as human beings are concerned, as far as their "appropriation" of this salvation is concerned—how they make it their own—the concrete tie is of an *ethical* character. God's salvation is always offered in history, but each human being must make it his or her own, and the way we do this is an ethical way. And so you always get a real, univocal equivalency—a concrete, one-for-one equivalency—between salvation and grace, for example, or salvation and virtue: love, justice, unselfishness, forgiveness, treating your neighbor as a brother or sister, and so on. And perdition, the opposite of salvation, always goes concretely one-for-one with sin, evil, or vice (selfishness, hatred, domination, wickedness, and so on).

In political terms, this means that salvation happens in liberation—so long as that liberation is the liberation of the oppressed: in other words, provided the political process leads to the creation of more humane and more humanizing structures. Therefore, as long as a liberation movement dignifies the oppressed person, it will always be a vessel of grace, and in this sense a "sacrament."

Priest.   Absolutely correct. The correspondence between salvation and liberation is of an ethical nature. It's not actually political. It's not "good politics" that makes the kingdom come, it's politics that's morally good, politics that's just. This means that there's no way you can draw up an equation between the kingdom and a historical success, or between sin and a historical failure. In this sense, history is profoundly ambiguous and always has to be sieved through the grid of ethical judgment. There are crimes that make history "advance," but not the kingdom, and vice versa.

Theologian.   Luther used an enlightening formula to show the difference, even the logical contradiction, between God's activity and human activity in history: he said they were *tecta sub cruce et contrario.* History is "covered, hidden, under the cross and its contrary."

Activist.   There's a popular saying that's just as good: "God writes straight with crooked lines."

Theologian.   Only, you can't make a reading principle out of this and systematically read every political victory as something negative as far as faith is concerned, and just the opposite, read every historical catastrophe as something positive in the eyes of God. This would lead to nihilism. It would be absurd.

Priest.   And there's another logic that's no good: Hegel's. He identified political success with giving glory to God, and failure with depriving God of it.

Theologian.   This is why we have to appeal to an ethical principle of interpretation. It's only when human beings win advancement and dignity—even if they perish in the effort—that there's a step forward in the direction of the kingdom. Whether you win or lose certainly has political importance, but either one can be a plus or a minus from the faith point of view. So an activist from among the people may die anonymously, but he or she doesn't die absurdly, from the faith viewpoint. An authentic, just, popular movement may be crushed, but it preserves its weight, it keeps its value, not only beyond this historical moment, but just plain beyond history—and independently of whether it's resurrected in history or not. The Paris Commune was resurrected by history, and keeps being resurrected by history. But how many movements have there been in history, inspired by justice, that have been buried forever, erased from human memory!

The Kingdom in the Infrastructure

Activist.   If I understand you correctly, God and God's kingdom act on the level of infrastructure too, for example, on the level of relationships of production, and even in the class struggle.

Theologian.   Unfortunately, we have a narrow view of Christianity, and especially of God. We think God acts only on the level of the heart, or of conscience. Actually, God is Lord of history. God acts through history, and through its laws, even though these laws seem to go directly against God and look as if they'd need a whole theodicy. After all, why should history slosh ahead with its feet mired in the infrastructure of economic production instead of with its head held high among ethical values and religious ideals? Why, in order to change, does society often have to pass by way of such dramatic, tragic confrontations, like all the different forms of class struggle, instead of strolling down the path of understanding, dialogue, and mutual love? There's a great deal to reflect on here. There's not much theology being done on the data Marxism has dug up. And not to have this theology is a lack that's starting to hurt.

Activist.   Then if history produces more justice, the kingdom is being actualized too.

Theologian.   So it would seem. It seems that in terms of the kingdom there's a process that passes by way of the mediation of these laws of history—and more or less unconsciously and involuntarily.

Priest.   But look, salvation doesn't act really all that anonymously and impersonally. The question is in whom, or to whom, this salvation is happening. After all, it's always concrete persons who are saved.

Theologian.   This is true. It happens to those who hear the call of the signs of the times and give themselves, make up their minds to participate in the process and then go ahead and do it, fight for the emancipation of the oppressed, and dedicate themselves to this sacred cause as best they can. They're the ones whom grace happens to, they're the ones given grace.

The kingdom comes for persons in their capacity as agents of history, not in their capacity as the beneficiaries or objects of historical transformations. In China there's been a whole liberation process from Western colonialism, and a regime has been set up that's raised the people's standard of living. All this certainly shows a passage of grace, but the grace has come to those who have entered into the process, not to those who have only been socially benefited by it—and by no manner of means has it come to those who have consciously opposed the liberation by digging in their heels when it comes to giving up their selfish privileges. The kingdom, in politics, is on the side of the subjects, the agents—not on the side of the objects.

It's the same thing with sin. When bosses exploit workers, and workers live in misery, that's sin, that's the antikingdom—but for the bosses, not for the workers. Well, it is for the workers too, insofar as they passively accept such a state of things, and insofar as they try to "make it to the top" on their own, and not in concert with the community.

Priest. But conversion is turning to God and laying your life on the line, in accordance with God's will. Following Jesus is believing in his word and imitating his actions. I don't see what this has to do with politics, or even with liberation.

Theologian. Here again we have to stay away from a language of identity pure and simple, like: "conversion *is* revolution." The correct grammar is the grammar of topical realization: "Conversion is realized by entering *into* the revolutionary process." For instance, we can say perfectly well: *only when* I move closer to the oppressed do I move close to God, whose image and "children of predilection" they are, God's favorite sons and daughters. And *only when* I'm loyal to my oppressed comrades am I faithful to my alliance, our covenant, with God. And *only when* I follow the poor am I following Jesus—which makes them a universal, absolutely necessary sacrament of salvation. And so on and so on.

Priest. Well, this is true. But we musn't forget that conversion, like sin, has an interior dimension, which the social or political dimension can't substitute for.

Theologian. No doubt. Speaking in more general terms, we can say that salvation, or grace, for a person or a community, is a process comprising several "moments" or aspects. It doesn't happen only in the heart, and it doesn't necessarily happen the way you think it will. There are certain dominant aspects today, (the political aspect) and high points (the "day of conversion") but it is a complex process.

Activist.   Conversion and Christian love have to prove themselves in life. It's in practice that they show whether they're authentic or not, even in political practice—and today, *especially* in political practice.

Theologian.   I'd go further. Life, practice, politics—these are not only a proof of the solid existence of an antecedent, interior reality. They aren't just the locus of verification of faith, for example. They are, it so happens, necessary moments in the realization, the actualization, of faith itself. Conversion, faith, *agape,* are real-ized, take flesh, in practices. I find that the idea of a "test" or "proof" is not very adequate for conveying the relationship between faith and life, politics included. It's better to speak of "moments" or aspects of the realization of faith—love, conversion, courage, hope, and so on.

Theology of Liberation: "Second Theology"

Priest.   This way of thinking, and solving theological difficulties. . . . Do you remember what you were talking about a little bit ago—new epistemological principles of theology? Does what you're now saying have anything to do with those new principles?

Theologian.   It surely does. Classic theology does not permit us to organize a cohesive discourse on the problem we have today: the political problematic, especially on liberation. The old theology was built in a sacral, religious world, where historical problems were not taken in their autonomy—not taken as secular problems. With the coming of a secular culture, one that impinged on general human awareness more and more, theology underwent a great crisis: a crisis in its very foundations—linked, of course, to the crisis of Christianity itself, as faith and as church. From that moment on, two large regions appeared in the field of theological reflection, and these regions were neatly distinguished from each other: the region of "religious realities," representing the problematic of classic theology: God, Christ, grace, the commandments, the virtues, and so on—and the region of "secular realities": science, technology, economy, sexuality, art, society, politics, and so on. Political theology is part of this second theological region. So it's called "second theology."

In our Latin America today, politics is expressed in the form of oppression and in the form of liberation. Political theology seeks to ponder, especially, the immense process of popular emancipation. And because this was a theology that wanted to be both rigorous and very much alive, it took the name of "liberation theology." So liberation, here, is both a theoretical subject and the political banner of a practical theology, both at the same time.

Priest.   Taking a position like that, this theology would find it hard to escape the reproach of sectarianism, it seems to me. And this would make it "schismatic." It represents a class interest: the interest of the oppressed. It's a lobby. Now, theology is theology, period. This theology-with-modifiers business—"liberation theology," "political theology," "theology of captivity," and this and that—is *partial* theology, right from the start, in both senses of the word "partial": it takes sides, and it's mutilated. To come in and start right off with a position like that is a contradiction of the very concept of theology. You've got a theology here that's leaning pretty far toward heterodoxy.

Theologian.   The theology of liberation is a theology that's trying to take its historical responsibility seriously. It's not a "different" theology in the sense of a theology contrary to some other theology. No, it's making an effort to respond to the vocation that was its from the very beginning: to "think through the faith" in terms of history and from within history. In this sense, there's really nothing to quarrel about, as far as the designation "theology of liberation" is concerned. Perhaps the time has come when we need no longer speak in these terms, but could simply say "theology." After all, any theology in our historical conditions today can be a theology at all only if it's a theology of liberation—

under pain of betraying its most traditional vocation, and so being seen for the ideology it is, that is, a theoretical system masking existent contradictions: in our case, the painful reality of our people.

In the beginning, the use of this label was fully justified. The task at first was to awaken theological thinking to a new problematic, and this marked it off from traditional theology, which no longer answered to the historical needs of the faith and thereby threatened to betray those needs. I think it probable that the label "theology of liberation" was justifiable as long as there was another theology that persisted in claiming exclusivity, orthodoxy, and completeness for itself, and opposed "liberation" theology.

Theoretical Logic of "Second Theology"

Activist.   After all we've said, I still think liberation is liberation, and no figures of speech or metaphors about it.

Priest.   And I still think it's that, plus a lot more. Liberation includes the kingdom of God. Otherwise it wouldn't be integral.

Theologian.   This isn't a yes-or-no question. The question here is to see how a "second theology" is articulated—especially a "political theology," and for us, a liberation theology.

Here is a way of setting up this articulation. For the theology of liberation, or, better, and more simply, for theology (all theology), liberation is taken as its subject, its raw material, or material object. In this sense, liberation is considered in all its density as a historical and political phenomenon: it's the movement of an oppressed people becoming conscious of its oppression and struggling to throw off the yoke of social domination. Liberation, for theology, is a *theologizandum*—something to be "theologized." There's nothing about liberation from sin yet, nothing about liberation for grace yet, or anything like that. Liberation here is taken in its whole density and richness, including recourse to the social sciences. At this stage, theology makes use of the social sciences perfectly freely. This is what we've come to call the "socio-analytic mediation."

Now, then, the subject's been set up. Now it's time for theology to *look inside* liberation, and search out its transcendent, supernatural, salvific dimension. Inside, I say—within it, present within it, not outside it, adventitious, slapped on or superimposed by Christian intention or prayer. But in order to be able to do this—in order to be able to perceive the salvific dimension in political liberation—theologians will need to know what salvation is. For this they will have to use "first theology." How will they be able to tell us, for example, that in this or that particular liberation process we find a deed of salvation, if they don't know what salvation means?

And so, you see, "second theology"—in our case, the theology of liberation—needs "first theology." It cannot do without it. "First theology" treats of the kingdom of God *in recto:* the kingdom of God as a reality essentially distinct from the reality our eyes can see in society. It is also distinct from what sociologists can tell us, can explain to us, using the tools of their particular science. Between what our human perception can grasp in society, and what our faith says about it, there's no proportion. The two dimensions in question are intrinsically incommensurate —although we can relate them in ethical terms, because in actuality they're intimately bound up with each other.

Priest.   But the liberation theologians have criticized traditional theology: they call it ideological.

Theologian.   The reason they've done this is not because traditional theology is incorrect, but because of its social function. The criticism was political, not theoretical—although they did not make a very clear distinction between the two orders when they made their criticism. If any of the liberation theologians claimed to reject classic theology wholesale, because they considered it passé, they were making a mistake—and contradicting themselves. Without classic theology, the theology of liberation itself would not be able to say anything. It's only on the basis of

"first theology"—with it and through it, as an operational tool—
that a liberation theology can be built.

So, for example, once I understand what the term "salvation"
means, I can use it, somewhat as a lamp, to understand the historical reality of liberation from a theological viewpoint, so that I
can now say: salvation is in liberation; or the kingdom of God is
(or isn't, and how, and for whom, and to what extent, and so on)
in the kingdom of human beings, or indeed in this concrete society.

In a nutshell: liberation is the raw material—the "material
theologized upon" (Althusser's first level)—and the term "salvation" operates here on the level of the means of production: it's
the "theologizing formality," as we might call Althusser's second
level.

First Illustration: The Great Commandment Today

Activist.   I'd like to get down to brass tacks. God's great
commandment today is the struggle of the oppressed, and solidarity with them.

Priest.   God's great commandment today is the one Christ
laid down: love of God and love of neighbor. And that's the only
thing it can be.

Activist.   But what does that mean today, to love God and
love your neighbor? Doesn't it mean taking up the cause of the
oppressed? Doesn't it mean struggling with them for their liberation? And to be effective, doesn't this love have to be channeled
through a labor union, a political party, an organization of the
people?

Theologian.   Actually you're expressing a concrete, historical judgment. We might say you're talking "second theology."
Factually, for you, love for God in our concrete historical and
social conditions concretely means participation in the struggles
of the oppressed. It's not a matter of dogmatics here—it's not a
matter of an abstract, absolute judgment. The judgment that the

great commandment today is love of God and neighbor is a judgment of this kind. And the judgment is expressed correctly as far as its denotation is concerned. Its direct meaning is correct. But its connotation—the meaning it implies—is no longer defensible today, because it appears to exclude the possibility that this love has to have a particular historical and social expression. The judgment is situated in "first theology." This theology speaks about absolute, abstract principles. These principles need to be mediatized, they need to be applied—to our concrete historical and social situation. Through this mediation, theology passes to the level of "second theology."

Priest.   If love of God and neighbor means struggling in the class organizations of the oppressed classes, then neither Jesus, nor the Apostles, nor the majority of Christians and saints of the past loved God and their neighbor.

Activist.   Yes, but they didn't live in our times. Persons live in different situations in history.

Theologian.   Obviously, what you are saying has a validity of a historical kind. It's a concrete application of a general, abstract principle. Therefore what you say is valid for us today, in a context of oppressed countries. Outside this context, obviously love for God and neighbor will take another form.

Second Illustration: The Kingdom of God Today

Activist.   If that's the way it is, then I say that today, for us, the kingdom of God, concretely, is socialism.

Priest.   I recall a remark by Maurice Clavel, the French philosopher, a convert, who died recently. Capitalism, he said, is in the devil's bag of tricks, part and parcel—but the devil's got more in there than capitalism. So, now, to say that capitalism is the devil and socialism is the kingdom of God seems to me a manipulation of the faith. It's reducing it to a concrete ideology, to a particular political approach. But the Christian faith is transcendent. It's not identifiable with any system.

Activist.   Right. Still, it is incarnate in history. Never in a perfect way, obviously. But in some manner or other, it's always incarnate. The kingdom of God for us today is socialism. Maybe yesterday it wasn't. Maybe it won't be tomorrow. But in our particular, concrete conditions, that's the way it expresses itself and takes shape. That's what I think.

Theologian.   Without a doubt, the kingdom of God is not adequately identifiable with any system, because it's transcendent. But it's always incarnate in history in some way or other. It's not definitively bound up with capitalism or socialism. No system totally corresponds to the kingdom of God. Let's not close history. But the kingdom of God is always found historically linked with existing social systems. The kingdom of God is transcendent—and *therefore* it's immanent at the same time.

Activist.   I agree with that. I'd only like to go back a minute to what you called "liberation rhetoric." A language of liberation has been circulated in the churches. But it's already starting to be drained of any content. It gets used every which way. Everything is liberating, everything is liberation. A meeting of charismatics is liberating—it liberates you from tension, anguish, and loneliness. Group therapy is liberating, too. And *then* you hear that Jesus Christ is the only liberator. Once again you've fallen into the "metaphorizing" trap. This metaphorical language hides the fact that the people, the organized people, is its own liberator.

Well, then, who's the liberator? Jesus Christ or the popular classes? It's hard to tell down from up any more. If you say Jesus Christ is the liberator, there's the danger the people will "depoliticize" popular movements. I'm even afraid that the vocabulary of liberation has become so full of meaningless words that you can't really use it any more. Maybe it'd be better to talk independence, or emancipation of the working class, or even revolution. Theologians and priests had better stop kidnaping words. They run them through their theological still and boil off any reality they might contain.

Third Illustration: Jesus Christ Liberator

Priest.   Saying "Jesus Christ is Liberator" is the same thing as saying "Jesus Christ is the Redeemer," or "Jesus Christ is the Savior." Here's the only difference: "liberator" is a more modern word, it's more suggestive, it has a higher charge of meaning. Didn't the first Christians do the same thing? Didn't they take the most expressive titles that were in vogue and apply them to Jesus? Isn't this the way it was with "Son of God," or "Lord," or "Savior," which were terms applied to gods and emperors in the political scene of the time? Then why can't we do the same thing?

Activist.   It's a complicated business, all right. I don't see how you can get away from metaphorizing. Maybe religion actually contains some mechanism for "de-realizing" things. Then I say, too bad for religion. It's open to the accusation of being an "opium of the people" once again. It seems as if the only thing it can do is camouflage reality and fool the public.

Priest.   But what's reality? Reality isn't only what you can see and do. It isn't only society and history and politics. What about supernatural reality? That's reality too. It's a much more real, and rich, reality than the reality of this empirical world, either personal or social. I'll even say that supernatural reality is the source and basis of material, historical reality.

Activist.   But I can't just ignore the reality of hunger, sickness, death. They're realities that are forced on me. After all, I *see* suffering and death. It's only the rich and powerful who don't feel these misfortunes, and don't hook them up with their own reality. Sometimes the poor become anesthetized, and end up distracting themselves from their sufferings by looking for a fantasy world.

Theologian.   It's possible to apply the term "liberator" to Christ, as Christians have always done. Still, we have to understand that today's culture is profoundly secular. Words have the semantic weight that they have. They offer a certain resistance to "transsemanticization"—to being made metaphors of, without thereby also exercising the ideological function of dissimulating, covering over, some reality or other. As far as I'm concerned, I'd say it'd be a good idea to keep the term that's already been coined and received in theological language, the term "salvation," to designate the mystery of God or Christ. This would be what Puebla calls liberation in its transcendent aspect—liberation from sin, or liberation for communion with God. Then the term "liberation" would be left with its autonomous, secular content. After all, this is the meaning it has in the language of the modern mind, especially the modern social mind.

Now, with these precisions, we can say "Jesus is Savior," but not "Jesus is Liberator." When we say "Jesus is Savior," it is a statement proper to "first theology." In a language corresponding to history, on the level of "second theology," the most we could say is "Jesus is Savior *through* the liberation undertaken by human beings"—because de facto, it happens that it's through the mediation of the liberation commitment that salvation happens in this case. If "liberation" is taken in the straightforward, concrete meaning proposed, then to say "Jesus is Liberator" becomes a strictly mythological statement, hence an absurd one.

Activist.   The people, organized, is the agent of history. Liberation is self-liberation.

Theologian.   This is a statement that an activist, or a social analyst, can make. It's a statement of the secular mind, of secular rationality. It's legitimate, but it's devoid of any theological relevance. The faith view is to see things from God's point of view. In the faith view, God is the subject, the agent, of everything. And so just as God creates the world, and the human race, and uses all sorts of mediations for it—the forces of nature, of history, and so on—so also in the political realm: God's action passes by way of the intermediation of political forces, including economic forces.

And so it's not just nature that's a sacrament of God—history is too. This is the way the men and women of the Old Testament read history, especially the prophets. Actually, they posited too close a bond, too immediate a bond, between historical events and God's activity. And so a particular plague, for instance, would be seen as ordained by God as a punishment for the sins of the people. Today we are more protective of the autonomy of earthly realities. We see a whole series of immediate, and then more mediate, causes. But a religious view will link everything finally to God.

Not that God is the last link in a whole chain of causality. No, God is not the terminal cause, the superagent. God acts *behind* all these physical and historical causalities, *through* them, *within* them. Obviously God acts in God's own way, according to God's own logic. And so the popular expression "God writes straight with crooked lines" is absolutely true.

And for a Christian, everything is referred to Jesus Christ— even, and especially, for us today, the movement of history, or the process of political liberation. Therefore, from the faith viewpoint, it is perfectly legitimate to say that Jesus is *Savior* by the fact of the impetus he gives to men and women to join in love with the oppressed, and to give their lives for their economic, political, and cultural liberation. Similarly, we can say that Jesus is *Liberator* from human slavery by the fact that it is ultimately he who rouses the oppressed to demand their rights and to assert themselves as human beings.

Jesus is Savior and Liberator at once, because here we're dealing with the same thing—even if it's the same thing differently— that is, depending on whether you view it from either of two inseparable orders of being and causality. The order of salvation prevails at the heart of liberation. And the order of liberation is wholly and entirely within the plan of salvation.

Insufficiency of the Chalcedonian Dialectic

Priest. Then this is the acceptable formula: salvation leads to liberation and liberation leads to salvation. The one involves the other.

Theologian. That formula seems clear and distinct. It belongs to what is called the "Chalcedonian dialectic." But this formula calls for closer examination. The two terms of the relationship are not proportional. In theology, you can't strictly say that liberation *has* a human, historical dimension. No, liberation *is* a human, historical reality, all metaphorizing aside. Now, salvation does indeed have a historical, social dimension, or meaning—it means precisely liberation. In exact theological terms, liberation is defined as the social or political dimension of salvation. The larger horizon is salvation. It's against that horizon that liberation is situated. Liberation doesn't embrace, cover, include salvation. Salvation includes liberation, penetrates it, and spills out beyond it on all sides. The broader reality—the "element" or "atmosphere" of liberation, is salvation.

Activist. We also have to say that liberation is the vehicle of the kingdom of God in history. It's in solidarity with the oppressed, and in the struggle for justice, that the love Jesus wanted to bring to earth flows. In other words, liberation has a profound meaning that no purely human vision can grasp. An agnostic or Marxist activist will not admit any of this. For them, the liberation process has a purely historical sense and nothing else.

But not for the Christian. The Christian speaks of a kingdom of God, salvation, eternal life, a communion of saints, a resurrection. This is the authentic, broader dimension of historical liberation. And in the same way, salvation is the transcendent dimension of liberation.

Theologian. But the word "dimension" is ambiguous— like "element," which can be used to mean the same thing. An element can be a totality within which certain things are situated: in other words, "element" can mean "sphere" or "atmosphere," as when we say: "He's in his element." But "element" can also be a part, a component, of some whole, some totality, as when we say "elements" in chemistry.

In the same way, "dimension" doesn't have the same semantic value in these two statements: "Salvation is the transcendent dimension of liberation" and "Liberation is an immanent—the political—dimension of salvation." In the first statement, "dimension" seems to mean "the element" in the sense of "the atmosphere," or the "horizon of meaning." But in the second statement, "dimension" seems to mean "component element" or "meaning" or "aspect" or "level" or "expression."

But apart from all this, what is important to understand is that salvation is the great reality within which liberation is situated. Liberation is theologically understandable only when it is referred to salvation. Liberation is the political "dimension" (an aspect, an expression, a concretization) of salvation. But the larger subject, the great theological matrix, in which like expressions are inserted, is God's salvation, God as Savior.

The Political: Dominant Aspect of Christian Faith Today

Priest. It's clear then: genuine liberation is completely in God, in God's plan of salvation. But salvation is not wholly and entirely within the ambit of liberation. Salvation is outside the political field, too. It's in the field of my own relationships with myself—in prayer, contrition, decision, intention, and so on. It's in the field of my interpersonal relationships, such as my relationships with my family, with my friends, with my enemies, with the destitute, the weak, the elderly, with children, with anybody who's helpless politically. If you reduce everything to politics you've got yourself a new dogmatics, a new orthodoxy, a new religion. And that'll give you totalitarianism. Politics is only one dimension of our life.

Reduce everything to politics and you're adopting a "germinal terrorism." You're sowing the seeds of a terrorism to follow. You won't be able to listen to Beethoven, because he's bourgeois. You won't be able to say grace before meals, because that's alienating. You'll have to worry about who is going to "bug" the conjugal bedroom to see if the love being made is reactionary or revolutionary. The same thing will happen in theology. You won't be able to read and study the mystical poetry of John of the Cross until it's been censored. The verses from the gospels that don't seem to run along the lines of your basic political preconception will be expunged.

This obsession with the political is a real sickness. It's a deformation of perception, a regular monster. Nietzsche would do a great job of describing the obsessed. I can see him picturing them as a great clenched fist, with two legs, no eyes, no ears, just holes where they should have been, and a big, bilious liver in place of a heart!

Activist.   Let's not exaggerate. This is the kind of caricature you'd get from those who feel threatened in their position. How about a caricature like this? The bourgeois class, all in the form of a big, grasping hand, stomach, and . . . well I won't mention the rest.

Theologian.   A theology that intends to think through liberation—a theology of liberation—has never defended, and never will be able to defend, a view of politics as the *only* dimension of the faith. It only emphasizes that this dimension is the *most important* one today. It is not the most important in itself, but only in the present historical circumstances, where peoples are crushed under the weight of oppression and wandering in search of bread and human dignity. This is not to say, then, that the political praxis of liberation is the only one. I am saying only that it ought to be the *dominant* dimension.

Priest.   There are certainly other dimensions of faith that are not political. And I'm of the opinion that the most important dimension of faith is the *religious* dimension.

Activist.   And I find that the most important thing in the Christian faith is not the religious part: prayer, Mass, the sacraments, and the rest. The Pharisees did things like that. And plenty of Pharisees are still doing them today. For Jesus, what counted was love, justice, sincerity. Christianity is praxis. He showed this over and over again: "It is mercy I desire and not sacrifice" (Matt. 9:13). And "None of those who cry out, 'Lord, Lord,' will enter the kingdom of God, but only the one who does the will of my Father in heaven" (Matt. 7:21).

Priest.   But you should love God first, and above all else. And your neighbor only after that. This is what Jesus said.

Activist.   But you love God *by* loving your neighbor, as

Saint John said. Not by spending all your time in church. That's not loving God. It's by coming to the aid of your brothers and sisters in need. It's by struggling for them, at their side.

Theologian.   The question here is not what dimension of faith is most important in itself. The question here is to discover what dimension of faith is most important *today*. You see, the accents, the dominant aspects, of faith have varied a great deal down through the history of Christianity. In the first three centuries, during the religious persecutions, the most important aspect of the gospel was a profession of faith in the pagan world. To deny your own faith was the supreme act of betrayal. Later, with the peace of Constantine, the great sin was heresy: having an erroneous faith. At the same time, the great act of betrayal for others was compromise with the status quo: the important thing became spirituality, and, even more, asceticism—flight to the desert, solitude, "overcoming yourself," mortifying your passions, and so on. In the Middle Ages, the dominant dimension of Christianity was penitence and penance. In the East, the emphasis that prevailed was on the divine liturgy, public worship, and mysticism. In the nineteenth century, to be a Christian was mainly to be a "practicing" believer, and fulfill all your "religious duties," and then give relief to those in need, especially by alms and works of generosity, "benefactions." And so on.

Today we accentuate the political aspect. In the future, under other conditions, it will surely be different. Who knows, in a classless society, perhaps the aspect of faith that will then be the most important may be the interior, mystical aspect, but in some other way.

The Political Alone: The Logic of Apocalypse

Priest.   But for many persons the political aspect is the only aspect. Everything in the faith that's not linked directly or indirectly with the political is left out of account and treated as irrelevant, or even as alienating. The reduction, the totalization, of faith in the political eventually destroys faith itself. Suppose that, tomorrow, the basic social problems would be solved. What will become of Christianity? Will it be abolished? Will it be extinguished and have no more meaning?

Activist. Let me say again, we're not talking about the *only* aspect of faith, we're talking about the main, the dominant aspect of faith. This mania for seeing a political Christianity as one-sided, reductive, ideological—this is a comfortable expedient, and a dishonest one, for disqualifying a committed faith. You can't talk about the political dimension of faith without someone—and always someone of the same class and social position—starting in about a "mere politicization of the faith," an ideologization of Christianity, a utilization of the gospel, and what not. This is the fruit of the boundless fear of the political implications of Christianity.

Theologian. There may be groups of politicized Christians who actually reduce the truth of the faith to its political aspect. But these groups are in the minority, and they don't have much influence. The great majority only give the impression of a reductionism—especially in the eyes of the socially powerful and privileged.

The tendency to reduce the whole potency of faith to the political is understandable when you're aware of the dramatic, poignant, tragic reality of the great masses of oppressed. Then everything leads to a kind of concentration of forces on this focal point: liberation. And that's because there's a kind of concrete concentration of social contradictions here. In these cases, as in our case, it's the political that parcels out the tasks to be performed. Even for faith. And when there are religious groups that show reactionary colors, then there's an even greater condensing of positions, a greater galvanization of forces.

When capitalism shows itself to be the "666" of the whore of Babylon, the war against capitalism turns out to be the coming of the kingdom. It's the schema of the Book of Revelation that's played out here. Evil has reached its paroxysm, and you look for one last, final apocalyptic confrontation of the forces of good and evil, and then the blessed millennium. This is more or less how, unconsciously, the logic of apocalypse is played out in some mentalities. But this isn't really the big danger today.

Priest. To heal this "big, bad world" syndrome, this extreme pessimism with respect to present society, with its fanaticism, sectarianism, totalitarianism, and all the other "isms," you need a little humor. Not that history shouldn't be taken seriously. But our own quirks play their role sometimes.

Really, there's nothing about the faith to justify this sort of *reductio ad unum.* I'd even say that even in our present situation, where liberation, or the political dimension of faith, is dominant, the other dimensions of faith continue to exist as well—perhaps less importantly, but no less really: the religious dimension, the interior dimension, the interpersonal, the festive, the esthetic dimensions, and so on. These deserve our attention too.

Activist. But that's all they deserve.

Priest. Because it's unacceptable to sacrifice values today in the struggle to gain them tomorrow. This would be a self-contradiction. You can't struggle for a society of brothers and sisters by adopting means that militate against a communion of brothers and sisters. Maritain used to say, means are ends in action. Socialism starts right now or it's not worth the trouble. If we're after a qualitatively distinct society, our own political organization had better be one in which we can live the values we seek for that society. Means have to be homogeneous with ends.

Activist. If you want wheat, you've got to sow seed. There's no way around that. But there's another face to this issue, and one that can't be ignored, if we want to be realistic. The grain of wheat has to die to produce the stalk. In an objectively contradictory situation, you can be obliged to practice "tough love," you have to love enough to spank. Any teacher or parent knows that. That's why, if we want to be able to create fellowship, there will be times when we're forced to use coercion. There will be struggles before there will be true peace. For that matter, there are certain situations that are more violent than the most violent struggles. Appearances deceive.

Revolution and Salvation

Priest.   I just want to say that a liberation movement has supernatural weight, any value in terms of salvation, only when it's consciously lived as such. There are plenty of liberation movements that don't have any larger dimension, that have no religious dimension. They're purely secular phenomena. Take the Russian revolution, for example, or the Chinese, or the Cuban. Those are revolutions carried out under the aegis of Marxist atheism. From this viewpoint they not only have no dimension of transcendence whatsoever, but we have to say they're actually antihuman.

Activist.   You're attending to one aspect only. You can't deny the positive things those revolutions have achieved, especially in the area of the most basic rights: food, clothing, housing, education, medicine, and so on. Is anybody going to deny that these deserve approval and respect? John XXIII said so in *Pacem in Terris*. Everything that is just and genuine comes from God, and is done under the inspiration of the Holy Spirit.

Priest.   But there are such horrible things going on in those revolutions!

Theologian.   What we're discussing here are principles. Now, if the kingdom—or salvation, or grace—passes by way of the actualization of a new society, it isn't going to depend on explicit consciousness of God or an explicit wish to do God's will. Here's God's plan: when we struggle on the side of human beings, especially for the oppressed, we're struggling on God's side, whether we like it or not, and whether we know it or not.

So it's not the presence of Christians in a historical movement that gives the movement its supernatural character. That depends on the ethical rectitude of those who undertake it. The presence of salvation in a historical liberation is something objective. What can vary is whether, in this or that particular liberation, salvation is being effectuated or is being canceled. That does indeed depend on human beings. But the plan of salvation itself does not depend on them. That depends on God, on God's will. All human history unfolds within the order of salvation—under the concrete sign of the salvation that is always offered, and is accepted or rejected in accordance with ethical practices.

Christian Presence in Politics

Activist.   We still have to see what importance it has whether Christians are present in the political struggle—what role they have in it as Christians.

Priest.   Obviously it's going to be some apostolic presence, a missionary presence. It's going to be to bear witness to the faith, to call those involved in political struggle to the joy of believing in Jesus Christ.

Activist.   Smells like proselytism to me. Christians will look as if they're mixed up in the liberation struggle just to round up parishioners. They'll look like some kind of profiteers. They'll be utilizing the struggle and its organization for the interests of their religious institution. The struggle itself is of no interest to them. The only thing that interests them is their chance to do some evangelization. The presence of Christians in the struggle will have the look of mere expediency, if not hypocrisy.

Theologian.   Christians' participation in a people's struggle is based on the intrinsic value of that struggle—which, as we've seen, has an objective divine dimension for a Christian. Any evangelizing, then, will have to be done right from within the struggle. It'll have to have its two feet planted squarely in the witness of disinterested dedication to the cause of justice. For light and strength, faith is a force of the first magnitude. It can function in the practices of the popular struggle under the form of inspiration, *ethos,* spiritual power, mystique. This is how faith can be lived by Christians who are right in the middle of the struggle, where it becomes salt and leaven for the struggle itself. It "radicalizes" your commitment.

So it isn't faith that gives a supernatural, divine meaning to the struggle. It's the other way around. It's the objective, intrinsic meaning that the struggle already has, that gives faith its strength and force. It's not because the Christian goes to battle animated by supernatural faith that the battle is sanctified. It's the other way around: it's because the struggle already contains a supernatural magnitude that the Christian goes into it animated by faith. God's action in history always anticipates the action of human beings. Before Christianity can be a mystique—a system of *motivations*—it has to be a wisdom, a *Weltanschauung*—a system of *meanings*. Then, flowing from both of these, it becomes a "religion"—a system of *symbols*. Christianity is first and foremost divine salvation; after that it's Christian faith; and finally it's church institution. In a context of political practice, Christian faith always acts as a leaven, in the sense that it strives to guarantee that a liberation movement move in the direction of the kingdom—that is, it tries to make sure that it unfolds in freedom, justice, and humanity.

Religion: Integral Part of Integral Liberation

Priest.   But there is no genuine liberation that does not include an explicit religious dimension. The objective presence of the supernatural dimension won't do it. If this constitutive dimension remains unconscious, something is lacking to the liberation. *Evangelii Nuntiandi* is very clear on this point. It even says that, without this overt religious dimension, temporal liberation simply misrepresents itself. Obviously, then, social liberation demands its religious dimension in order to be *integral*. Otherwise it ceases to be genuine human liberation—liberation of the whole person and every person.

Theologian.   The religious dimension is certainly *essential* to liberation for it to be integral. Therefore a liberation that didn't involve this religious aspect, or, worse, that repressed it, would become antihuman and enslaving.

Activist.   By religion, of course, we mean something very precise here. We mean a public expression of faith. In that case it's true: it constitutes a dimension of social life itself—and a necessary dimension, right alongside the others: the economic, the political.

Priest.   But the religious dimension is different from those other dimensions. Religion, both in its practice and its form, belongs essentially to the reign of liberty. An integrally liberated society is not the one that adopts or imposes a particular, definite religion, but one that guarantees everyone a religious social space—the exercise of the right of religion.

Theologian.   When we speak of religion in these terms, in the way we're talking now, we're still on our homogeneous plane—we're still in the social and historical field. You might say religion is taken here in its purely social aspect.

Activist.   Well, it's as a social thing that religion is part of integral liberation. Religious liberation takes its place alongside political liberation. That's how religious liberation is an integral part of social liberation.

Liberation: Integral Part of Objective Salvation

Priest.   It's different, though, in the case of salvation. Then we're dealing with a "higher order," as Pascal said. Here there's a real ontic switch, an ontological rupture, or breach. Now we're in an order of reality where the only adequate language is that of faith and theology.

Theologian.   We've seen how this language operates, though. It seeks to comprehend the transcendent reality of salvation through metaphors in "first theology," and then tries to see how and where this salvation unfolds within the movement of history—including, and for us in Latin America today, especially, in the process of the emancipation of the oppressed—in "second theology," or liberation theology.

In the ontic order in which we were speaking of religion before, religion fell on a *horizontal line with political liberation;* whereas in this second order, religion, the "sacrament" of liberation, falls on a *vertical line with salvation.* This last order of reality is actually the supernatural, divine, salvific order, and no longer the social, human order, the order of liberation—although the supernatural order is present in this natural order.

Priest.   The magisterium and the theologians always include the religious aspect when they talk about "integral liberation."

Theologian.   Unfortunately, in their vocabulary, "religion" really has a double meaning. They're not distinguishing between the *socio-religious,* or sociological, aspect of religion, and its *supernatural,* or theological, aspect. They confuse the two orders we are speaking of: the orders of the signifier (the social) and the signified (the divine). Then what happens is, in order to have integral liberation, they issue an indiscriminate call for grace and religion, God and the church. Actually, religion as church is part of society, whereas God's grace is in no way any such part: it is a "principle," present (positively or negatively) in every society, Christian and non-Christian, and in all society—in economics as much as in religion considered socially.

Priest.   But it's the church that manifests this presence of salvation in the world, including its presence within liberation where it is present, by being a "sacrament of salvation."

Activist.   Of course. But the church has no monopoly on this presence, or on spreading it.

Theologian.   We could sum it up in this way: integral social liberation must always and necessarily include religion in the social sense (in our case, the church) as one of its parts. And at the same time, this same (integral) liberation includes salvation, includes God, but not as one of its parts—as its divine dimension, as its eschatological horizon.

Integral Liberation: The Role of the Church

Activist.   I don't see where you think you'll get with all these distinctions.

Priest.   Right—what concrete pastoral implications does all this have?

Theologian. Here are the implications. The pastoral efforts of the church mustn't directly aim at baptizing, sanctifying, or supernaturalizing human liberation—mustn't aim at adding a supernatural meaning to it. No, this is God's part. God has always raised the history of human beings to the level of divine history. And human beings—all human beings—respond to this "proffer of salvation" by being just and good, or unjust and evil. The first duty of the church is something else: grace. The first duty of the church is to guarantee, in history, the socio-religious aspect of liberation, which is where God's salvation manifests itself. And so its mission is based on the level of history, even though its final objective is transhistorical salvation.

Priest. The common position today, with the magisterium as with the theologians, is that liberation is integral only if it includes communion with God, and this communion with God is the work of the word and sacramental ministry of the church.

Theologian. This position should be submitted to a more rigorous examination. It neglects two basic facts. First, communion with God, or grace, is a possibility intrinsically available to society itself, to history itself, to political practice, and it can occur outside the church just as it occurred before there ever was a church. In other words, social liberation already contains the element of salvation, even antecedently to the intervention of the church or indeed without that intervention.

Secondly, the role of the church, when it comes to conferring an integral dimension on historical liberation, consists precisely in this: in assuring the socio-religious aspect of human liberation, and in thereby guaranteeing the Christian mystique of politics—and finally, in assuring in this way the positive presence of grace at the heart of historical liberation. Accordingly, the role of the church as sacrament of salvation in the history of liberation is not to produce grace, but to guarantee it—to see that grace arrives at its destination.

Priest. In that case, the church isn't necessary for salvation. You could just as well get along without it. Your position is contrary to traditional doctrine, as based on scripture.

Activist.   But you can see in scripture that there was grace before there was a church, and that there's grace today outside the church.

Theologian.   The presence of the church in history is not what is called "absolutely" necessary: it's "morally" necessary —historically necessary, then, given the concrete human condition from the viewpoint of salvation. This situation—a "moral" necessity that salvation should come via the church—flows ultimately from original sin. The church is necessary on the level of the historical *conditions* of the "production of grace," rather than on the level of the instrumentality of this "production." The church isn't a machine for making grace—it's part of the ambient, the circumstances of grace.

Activist.   But we're getting away from the point.

Priest.   This is a good example of how everything in theology is connected to everything else. You can't handle the subject of liberation theology adequately without touching on these classic questions treated by any good theology.

Theologian.   Perhaps we can sum up the discussion we've had on integral liberation and on where the church fits in, in this way: the mission of the church, as sacrament, is to *integrate* social liberation—horizontally—by publicly proclaiming and celebrating, in sacrament and sign, the fact that social liberation *intrinsically* integrates salvation—vertically. Why? Because this social integration guarantees the supernatural integration of human liberation, on the level of sacramental instrumentality.

Levels of the Relationship between Christianity and Liberation

Activist.   I think that the mission of the church is more than just to guarantee the religious part of integral liberation. That's the old "sacristy church," and we've gotten beyond all that forever—to the discomfiture of the dominant classes.

Theologian.   I think we have to distinguish here between the church and Christians. The church as institution, as public manifestation, seems to me to be limited to the religious area in the narrow sense, the "sacramental" area. The church will either be speaking in a religious manner about the political, or it will be celebrating liturgically the salvation that occurs in the political. This role is performed primarily by the ministers of the church, especially by the hierarchy. This, I say, is properly the role of the institutional church.

But with Christians as such it's a different matter. They act in the political arena side by side with others—only, they do this with their own mystique, their own "spirituality," with the inspiration they draw from faith, from the gospel. This is their contribution to the salvation of the human being—for, in the measure that human beings open themselves to justice and love, they are—even without knowing it—accepting and embracing the kingdom, grace, and Jesus Christ.

Priest.   In other words, there are different levels in the so-called relationship of faith and politics.

Theologian.   Exactly. I think you could sum up all three levels *in globo* by calling the relationship "Christianity and liberation." Then, to distinguish the levels, we would say that the first level, the most superficial one, consists in the *liberation-religion* relationship, which is an "instituted," an institutional, relationship, whose agent is the *church*. Then there's the second level, the intermediate one, the level of the *liberation–Christian faith* relationship, which is a relationship lived by *Christians as such*. Finally, on the third level, the deepest level, there's the *liberation-salvation* relationship which is an objective relationship, *decreed by God* whether or not it's accepted by the ethical practice of human beings.

Activist.   Look, I don't want to know how many angels can dance on the head of a pin. We've already made enough distinctions. These things all have to be worked out in practice. As the farmers say: "Get the wagon going! Then the potatoes'll settle."

Priest.   As far as I'm concerned, I think it's important to clear up all these points, otherwise Christian teaching can be misinterpreted.

Theologian. You can see from this that a simple theology won't do when it comes to answering the burning questions that arise from Christians' political commitment. We need a richer, deeper theology than any we've had until now. In that way we'll be prepared to "give an account of our faith" at the heart of the concrete confrontations of our time. This is what Saint Peter recommends, and this is what theology has always reckoned as its proper task.

Summation

Activist. Why don't we make a list of the points that have become clear in our discussion?

Priest. That would be a good idea.

Theologian. I'd summarize them in this way:

1) We must come right out and say it, loud and clear: *liberation is the social emancipation of the oppressed.* Our concrete task is to replace the capitalist system and move toward a new society—a society of a socialistic type.

2) Social liberation, however, is never merely social. It is lived and experienced as a deeply meaningful phenomenon, open to transcendence, and therefore involving a transhistorical reference that revelation calls salvation or the kingdom of God.

3) But this salvation, this kingdom, is to be found *within* the process of liberation—although only when this process is morally good—that is, humanizing.

4) Faith gives us to perceive this mysterious presence of salvation within liberation, and theology seeks to express it in a critical and methodical way, a rigorous and systematic fashion.

5) Salvation is not to be found only in liberation, but liberation is the most important locus of its concretization, liberation is its *dominant dimension* in the context of our concrete situation today, in our dependent Latin America.

6) Our faith, as professed in the church and lived out in practice, is *necessary* in our concrete history, as a guarantee that liberation will move in the direction of the kingdom, in the direction of salvation.

Notes

1. References to the Puebla Final Document are to John Eagleson and Philip Scharper, eds., *Puebla and Beyond: Documentation and Commentary* (Maryknoll, N.Y.: Orbis, 1979), citing paragraph no.

2. See Joseph Gremillion, *The Gospel of Peace and Justice: Catholic Social Teaching since Pope John* (Maryknoll, N.Y.: Orbis, 1976), p. 395.

3. See ibid.

4. The best work on this subject is that by Clodovis Boff, *Teologia e prática: Teologia do político e suas mediações* (Petrópolis: Vozes, 1978), to be published in English by Orbis Books.

5. For a historical examination of the theology of liberation, see Alfonso Garcia Rubio, *Teologia da libertação: Política ou profetismo?* (São Paulo: Loyola, 1977); Roberto Oliveros Maqueo, *Liberación y teología: Génesis y crecimiento de una reflexión, 1966-1977* (Lima: Centro de Estudios y Publicaciones, 1977); Edward L. Cleary, *Crisis, Change, and the Church in Latin America* (Maryknoll, N.Y.: Orbis, forthcoming).

6. Luiz Gonzaga de Souza Lima, *Evolução política dos católicos e da Igreja no Brasil: Hipóteses para uma interpretação* (Petrópolis: Vozes, 1979).

7. See Gustavo Gutiérrez, *A Theology of Liberation* (Maryknoll, N.Y.: Orbis, 1973), pp. 145-87.

8. See Leonardo Boff, *Teologia do cativeiro e da libertação* (Lisbon: Multinova, 1976), pp. 57ff.

9. Comisión Episcopal de Acción Social, *Signos de renovación* (Lima: CEP, 1974), p. 47.

10. The highlights of this paragraph (no. 39) of *Gaudium et Spes* are: "What was sown in weakness and corruption will be clothed with incorruptibility. While charity and its fruits endure, all that creation which God made on man's account will be unchained from the bondage of vanity. . . . The expectation of a new earth must not weaken but rather stimulate our concern for cultivating this one. For here grows the body of a new human family, a body which even now is able to give some kind of

foreshadowing of the new age. . . . For after we have . . . nurtured . . . all the good fruits of our nature and enterprise, we will find them again, but freed of stain, burnished and transfigured. This will be so when Christ hands over to the Father a kingdom eternal and universal. . . . On this earth that kingdom is already present in mystery. When the Lord returns, it will be brought into full flower" (in Gremillion, *Gospel of Peace and Justice*, pp. 273-74).

11. English translations are taken from *On Evangelization in the Modern World* (Washington, D.C.: USCC, 1976).

12. See Karl Lehmann et al., *Theologie der Befreiung* (Einsiedeln: Johannes Verlag, 1977), esp. pp. 173ff.

13. *SEDOC* (Petrópolis), 10 (1978) 744.

14. "The declaration of the International Theological Commission fell far short of *Gaudium et Spes*, Medellín, and the Synod of Bishops. A European ought to recognize that Latin American theologians have reason to be simply furious about this" (José Ignacio González Faus, "La declaración de la comisión teológica internacional sobre la teología de la liberación," *Christus* [Mexico City], 43 [1978] 21).

15. New York, Seabury, 1970.

16. See Gustavo Gutiérrez, *The Power of the Poor in History* (Maryknoll, N.Y.: Orbis, 1983), chap. 5, "The Preparatory Document for Puebla: A Retreat from Commitment," pp. 111-24.

17. *Veja*, no. 543.

18. "Opening Address at the Puebla Conference," III, 6, in Eagleson and Scharper, *Puebla and Beyond*, p. 68, citing *Evangelii Nuntiandi*, no. 9.

19. Ibid.

20. Ibid., I, 8 (Eagleson and Scharper, *Puebla and Beyond*, p. 62).

21. *Juan Pablo II, peregrino de la fe: Documentos* (Mexico City, 1979), p. 112; italics added.

22. "Address to the Indians of Oaxaca and Chiapas," in Eagleson and Scharper, *Puebla and Beyond*, p. 82.

23. Ibid.

24. Ibid; see also "Opening Address," III, 4 (Eagleson and Scharper, pp. 67-68).

25. "Address to the Indians" (Eagleson and Scharper, p. 83).

26. See "Opening Address," III, 3 (Eagleson and Scharper, p. 66).

27. See Ibid., 2, 4 (Eagleson and Scharper, pp. 66, 67).

28. *Redeemer of Man*, (Washington, D.C.: USCC, 1979), no. 12, p. 36.

29. Ibid., no. 9, pp. 25-26.

30. *Osservatore Romano*, Italian edition, Feb. 22, 1979, pp. 1-2.

31. Ibid.

32. Ibid.

33. See Leonardo Boff, "Puebla: ganhos, avanços, problemas emergentes," *Revista Eclesiástica Brasileira* (*REB*), 39 (March 1979).

34. See Ronaldo Muñoz, "Comentário ao capítulo eclesiológico do Documento final de Puebla," *REB*, 39, 113ff.

35. See Ronaldo Muñoz, *Nova consciência da Igreja na América Latina* (Petrópolis: Vozes, 1979).

36. See note 4, above. See also, by the same author, *Comunidade eclesial—comunidade política: Ensaios de eclesiologia política* (Petrópolis: Vozes, 1978).

37. *Teologia e prática*, pp. 14, 17.

38. Ibid., pp. 281-303.

39. Ibid., pp. 67-68, 112-30.

40. Ibid., pp. 131-272; Leonardo Boff, *Teologia do cativeiro*, pp. 36ff., 57-58.

41. Clodovis Boff, *Comunidade eclesial*, p. 14.

42. In Gremillion, *Gospel of Peace and Justice*, p. 261.

43. Ibid., p. 274.

44. See Clodovis Boff, *Teologia e prática*, pp. 273-376.

45. Henricus Denzinger and Adolfus Schönmetzer, *Enchiridion Symbolorum, Definitionum et Declarationum de Rebus Fidei et Morum* (DS) (Barcelona, Freiburg, and Rome: Herder, 1976). See also José Ignacio Gonzáles Faus, "Las fórmulas de la dogmática cristológica y su interpretación actual," *Estudios Eclesiásticos*, 46 (1971) 339-67.

46. See Leonardo Boff, "O que significa propriamente Sacramento?" *REB*, 34 (1974) 860-95.

47. Document presented by the bishops of West Germany, Feb. 21, 1963, as a contribution to the Dogmatic Constitution on the Church. See the analysis in Leonardo Boff, *Die Kirche als Sakrament im Horizont der Welterfahrung* (Paderborn: Bonifacius, 1972), pp. 250-57.

48. In Gremillion, *Gospel of Peace and Justice*, p. 254.

49. *Gaudium et Spes*, no. 39 (in Gremillion, *Gospel of Peace and Justice*, p. 274).

50. Ibid., no. 39 (Gremillion, p. 273).

51. Ibid., no. 38 (Gremillion, p. 273).

52. Ibid., no. 38 (Gremillion, pp. 273).

53. Ibid., no. 39 (Gremillion, p. 273-74).

54. Ibid.

55. Ibid.

56. Ibid.

57. Sermon 362, 7.

58. *Gaudium et Spes*, 39, 43 (in Gremillion, *Gospel of Peace and Justice*, pp. 273-74, 278).